SEVEN ON A MAT

A Story of Faith, Luck and Courage
During World War II

by
Doris Mayberry

with
Owen Mayberry

© 2020 Candace Joan Mayberry

Published by
Ontario History Press
to commemorate the
75th Anniversary of VE Day

2020

To commemorate the 75th Anniversary of
Victory in Europe Day (1945 - 2020),
this limited edition of
SEVEN ON A MAT
has been published by

Ontario History Press
with the advice and guidance of
The Prince Edward Historical Society
Prince Edward County, Ontario, Canada.

Written by Doris Mayberry
with Owen Mayberry

Foreword by Candace Joan Mayberry

Edited by Marc Seguin
marc@ontariohistory.ca

© 2020 Candace Joan Mayberry

All rights reserved. No part of this publication may be reproduced, stored in a retrieval system or transmitted in any form or by any means, electronic, mechanical, photocopying, recording or otherwise, without the prior written consent of the copyright holder.

ISBN: 978-0-9940106-5-0

This book is available at local bookstores, online, or from
The Prince Edward Historical Society
Ontario, Canada
www.pehistsoc.wordpress.com

Cover design by Marc Seguin © 2020
The background image shows a portion of The Netherlands from a WWII "silk" escape map. The back cover includes the flag of Holland together with the uniform wing patches of the seven Allied airmen:
RAF pilot, three USAAF pilots, USAAF bombardier/togglier,
RAAF wireless operator/airgunner, RCAF pilot.

Table of Contents

Foreword	1
Editor's Note	3
Reference Maps	7
Glossary	13

Dedication		19	7 Life at Somsenhuis	89
Preface		21	8 Christmas and the New Year	96
Background: The Seven Allied Airmen		23	9 Plans	101
			10 Jim's Story	105
1	Owen's Story	25	Jim's Rescue	111
	Owen's Rescue	30	11 Chuck Arrives	117
2	Ted	36	12 Danger!	119
3	Ted's Story	41	13 Chuck's Story	125
4	The Farm Somsenhuis	46	14 The Silent Seven	128
5	Frank's Story	56	15 March 30, 1945	130
	Joe	61	16 Doris's Story	141
6	Bobby's Story	69		
	The Bluff	73	Epilogue	146
	Hospital	76	Authors' Notes	161
	Plans for Escape	77		
	Bobby's Rescue	81		

Index	165

Illustrations

Papa and Moeder Prinzen	19
2nd Lt. Owen L. Mayberry	25
Somsenhuis 1944-45	51
"De Bark" 1945	53
The Prinzen Family c.1945	88

FOREWORD

by Candace Joan Mayberry

This is my father's memoir of how seven Allied airmen came to be hidden in the attic of a farmhouse belonging to the Prinzen family in Nazi-occupied Holland during World War II. Along with the aid of the Dutch Underground, these men were saved from capture by the German Army. The bravery and discipline shown by the Prinzen family and members of the Underground was exemplary.

It all came about when the planes of each of the seven airmen were hit with flak from German anti-aircraft guns or shot down by enemy fighter planes during their missions over Germany. They had to bail out quickly, or die!

Each man's story is told in rich detail about the dangers they went through before arriving at the farmhouse. Each flyer was given farm work to do, along with helping the Underground, giving them something productive to occupy themselves and to feel like they were contributing. The farm produced enough food to feed everyone in spite of what was sometimes taken by the Germans. There were "white knuckle" moments though. One time, the Germans just walked into the farmhouse, without knocking, as a family member was handing food up to the flyers or taking a latrine bucket down. At another time there were German officers living downstairs at the farmhouse while the airmen were shuttered up in the attic. If the Prinzens had been caught hiding Allied soldiers, the whole family would have been shot!

In spite of the dangers, there was laughter and love. A strong bond was formed between the airmen and the family. After the war, most of the Prinzens immigrated to Canada and the airmen returned to their respective countries to raise families and to enjoy life.

This story was written in 1994 and 1995 by my mother, Doris Mayberry, as told to her by my father, Owen Mayberry, along with extensive research to get the stories of the other six men. This was one of the most important events in my father's life. My parents kept in touch with the Prinzens through the years and visited them several times in Canada. They also visited the Netherlands to see former members of the Dutch Underground. The Dutch were, in turn, grateful for what men like my father did to free their homeland. My parents never forgot what the Prinzen family did to save these men.

This book is my parents' legacy.

Candace Joan Mayberry
Sacramento, California
2020

Editor's Note

Under dire circumstances after the end of World War II, the Prinzen family emigrated from war-ravaged Holland to the tranquil farming community of Prince Edward County, Ontario, Canada. They brought with them the remarkable story of how they had worked with the Dutch Underground to shelter seven downed Allied airmen in occupied Holland during the last few months of the war.

Some fifty years later, Doris Mayberry, the wife of one of the airmen, 2nd Lt. Owen L. Mayberry, USAAF, recorded the experiences of these airmen and of this courageous family and produced the initial manuscript of "Seven On A Mat".

In 2020, on the eve of the seventy-fifth anniversary of Victory-in-Europe Day (VE Day), the youngest of the Prinzen children, Benny, who at age four had been an active participant in the wartime events in Holland described in "Seven On A Mat", passed on a copy of Doris Mayberry's manuscript to the Prince Edward Historical Society. To commemorate the VE Day anniversary, the Historical Society sought to have the manuscript published.

Sadly, Doris Mayberry had passed away in 2012, and Owen Mayberry had passed away eight years earlier. Fortunately, the Historical Society was able to connect with their daughter, Candace Joan Mayberry of Sacramento, California, and she has very kindly given her permission to have this limited edition of "Seven On A Mat" published..

Beginning in May, 1940, and throughout the remainder of the Second World War in Europe, Bomber Command of Britain's Royal Air Force directed thousands of bombing raids against German targets. By 1942, the number of raids increased dramatically when the United States' 8th Air Force (initially the U.S. VIII Bomber Command) joined the battle.

Canada, far from the front lines, contributed to the airwar in Europe by building aircraft, supplying airmen and training thousands of pilots and aircrew as part of the British Commonwealth Air Training Plan (BCATP). During the war, several of the hundreds of Canadian BCATP training facilities were located in and around Prince Edward County, Ontario. These included a Bombing and Gunnery School at the Picton aerodrome, and another Bombing and Gunnery School at the Mountain View aerodrome along with the Air Armament School. The Central Flying School together with a Flying Instructor School, an Air Navigation School and a Repair Depot were located at the Royal Canadian Air Force base in nearby Trenton. There was also an Initial Training School in Belleville for pilots and navigators, and the Instrument Navigation School in Deseronto.

In June, 1944, 'Operation Overlord' — D-Day — the Allied invasion of Normandy, marked the beginning of the tumultuous eleven-month period that would bring an end to the war in Europe with the surrender of the German forces in May, 1945. During these last months of the war, the German Army was relentlessly pushed back on the ground by the advancing Allied armies. The 1st Canadian Army, composed of several British and Canadian divisions, fought their way through Holland, liberating town after town. Among the Canadian soldiers were many Prince Edward County boys serving with the Hastings and Prince Edward Regiment.

In the air, the Allied air forces continued their around-the-clock bombing raids against German targets; the Americans flying missions during the day and the British and Commonwealth squadrons flying at night. Over the course of more than five years of war and many thousands of bombing missions, many Allied aircraft and their crews were shot down by German anti-aircraft fire or by German fighter planes. Many of the aircrew did not survive. Others parachuted to relative safety only to be captured and imprisoned — or shot — by the German Army. Still others, a small percentage of the total number of downed flyers, managed to evade capture and either make their way back to the Allied lines or go into hiding until the Germans retreated or surrendered.

At great risk to their own lives and to the lives of their ten children, Bernard and Dora Prinzen harboured seven of these downed airmen for several months before they were liberated by advancing Allied ground forces in March, 1945.

As of 2020, several of Bernard and Dora's children, along with more than one hundred of their descendants, still live in Prince Edward County, and dozens more live in the surrounding area and throughout other parts of Canada.

In an attempt to add greater clarity to the events and places described in this book, some minor editorial changes have been made to the original 1995 manuscript. These include updating the spelling of place names, correcting the names of some of the participants and adding a few minor editorial comments [shown in square brackets], along with footnotes and several maps and photographs which were not part of the original copy. Nothing has been left out from Doris's original manuscript.
While the book is written from Owen Mayberry's perspective, and largely narrated in Owen's voice, each airman narrates his own story. In order to avoid confusion, whenever narration switches from Owen, or back to Owen, the symbol • • • has been inserted between paragraphs.

Thanks are due to the Executive Committee of the Prince Edward Historical Society — Lorri Busch, Peter Jepson, Sandy Latchford, Mary Lazier, Molly McGowan, Fergus Millar and Barbara Sweet — for supporting this project, with special thanks to Mary Lazier for her untiring proofreading efforts and editorial suggestions.
Further thanks are due to Ben Prinzen and the Prinzen family of Prince Edward County, Ontario, for their help and support, also to Charles Burbank of Kingston, Ontario, Canada, and Monica Walsh of the Royal Australian Air Force Museum, Victoria, Australia, for consulting on technical aspects of the manuscript, and to Marjorie Seguin for her insightful editorial comments and additional proofreading.
Also, many thanks to Candace Joan Mayberry for writing the Foreword and for allowing this book to be published.

Marc Seguin
Vice-President,
Prince Edward Historical Society
May 8, 2020

Reference Maps

Map 1 --- **Western Europe, 1944.**
Adapted from "Allied Invasion of the Western Front, Hitler's Inner Fortress", U.S. Office of War Information, *A War Atlas for Americans*, New York, 1944.

(The area marked by the dashed rectangle ⌐ ¬ is shown in larger scale on Map 2.)

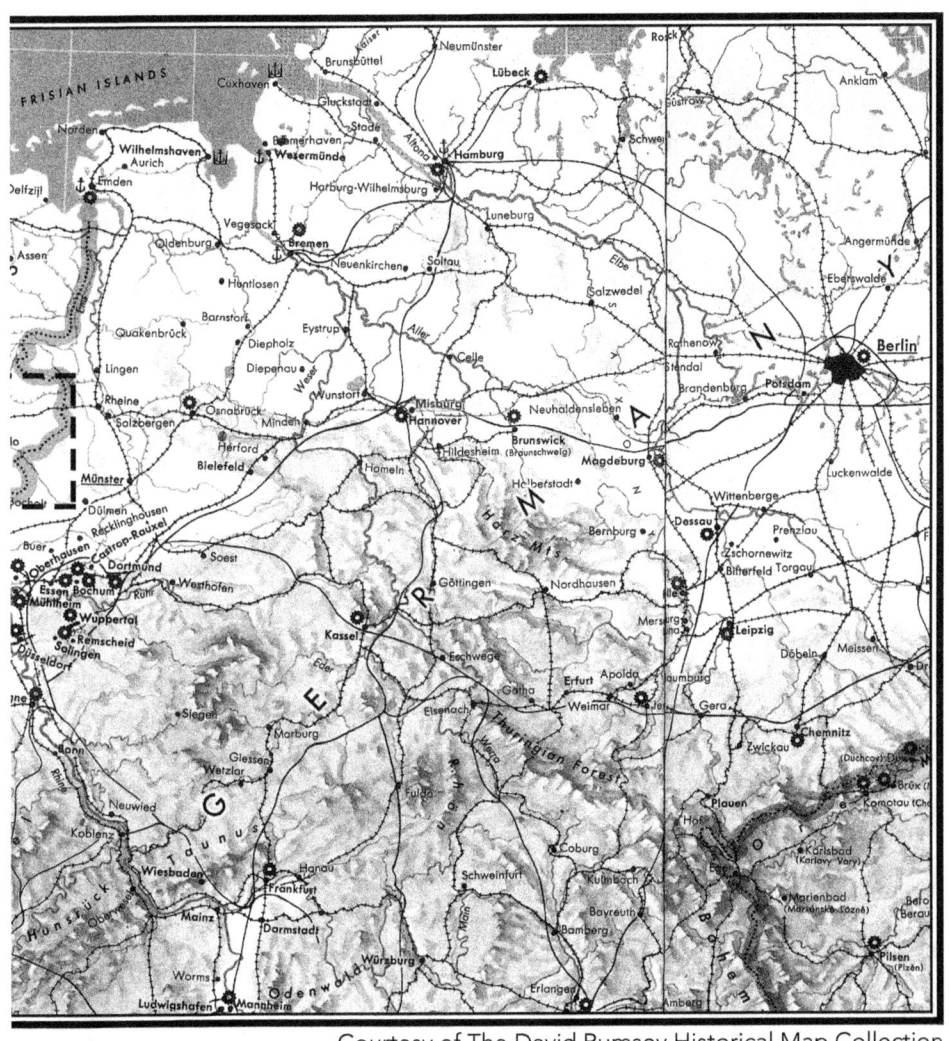

Courtesy of The David Rumsey Historical Map Collection
Adapted by Marc Seguin, 2020

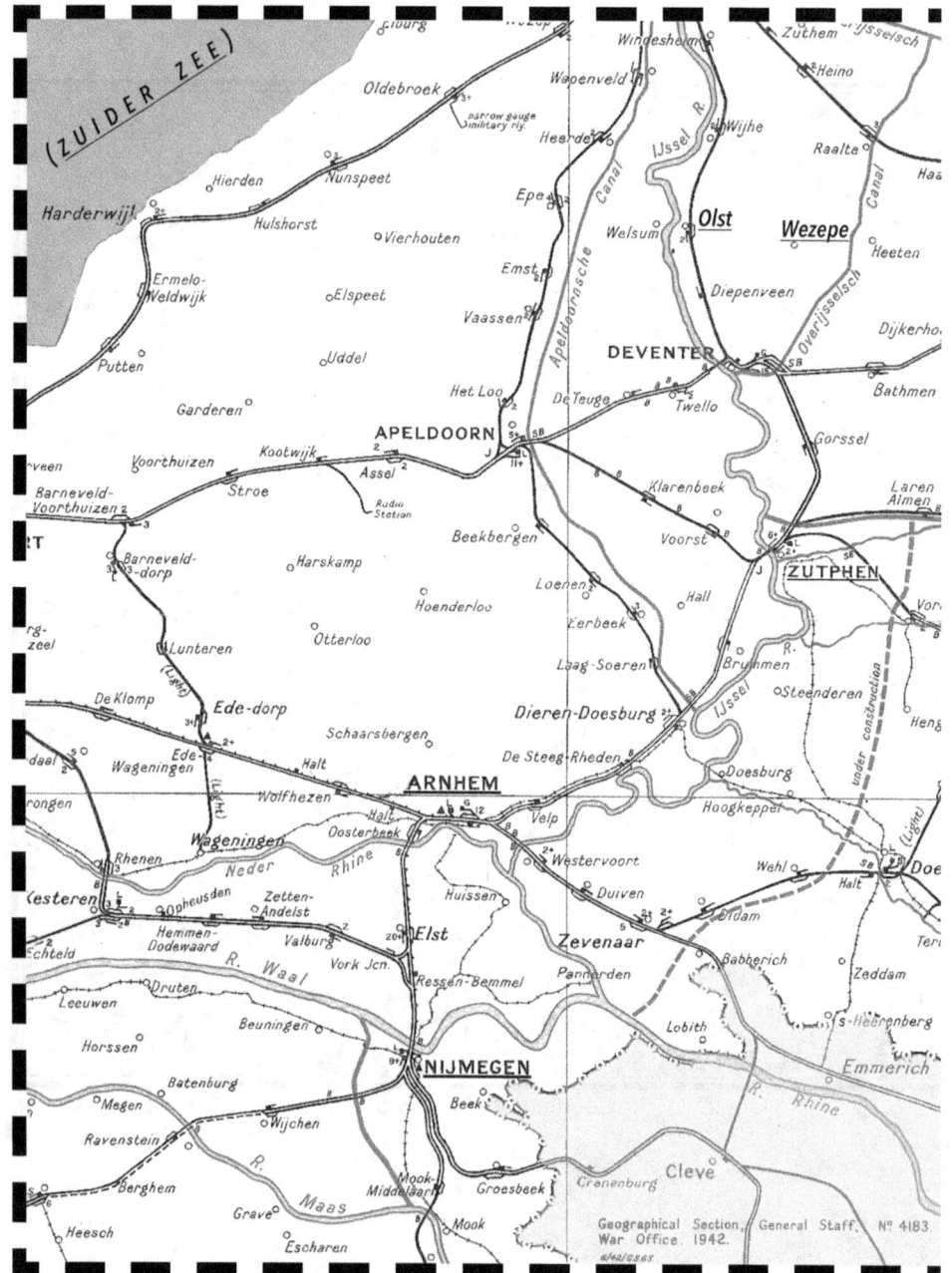

Map 2 --- **Eastern Holland, 1943**.
Adapted from *Railways and Waterways of Holland*, Great Britain, War Office, General Staff Geographical Section, London, 1943.

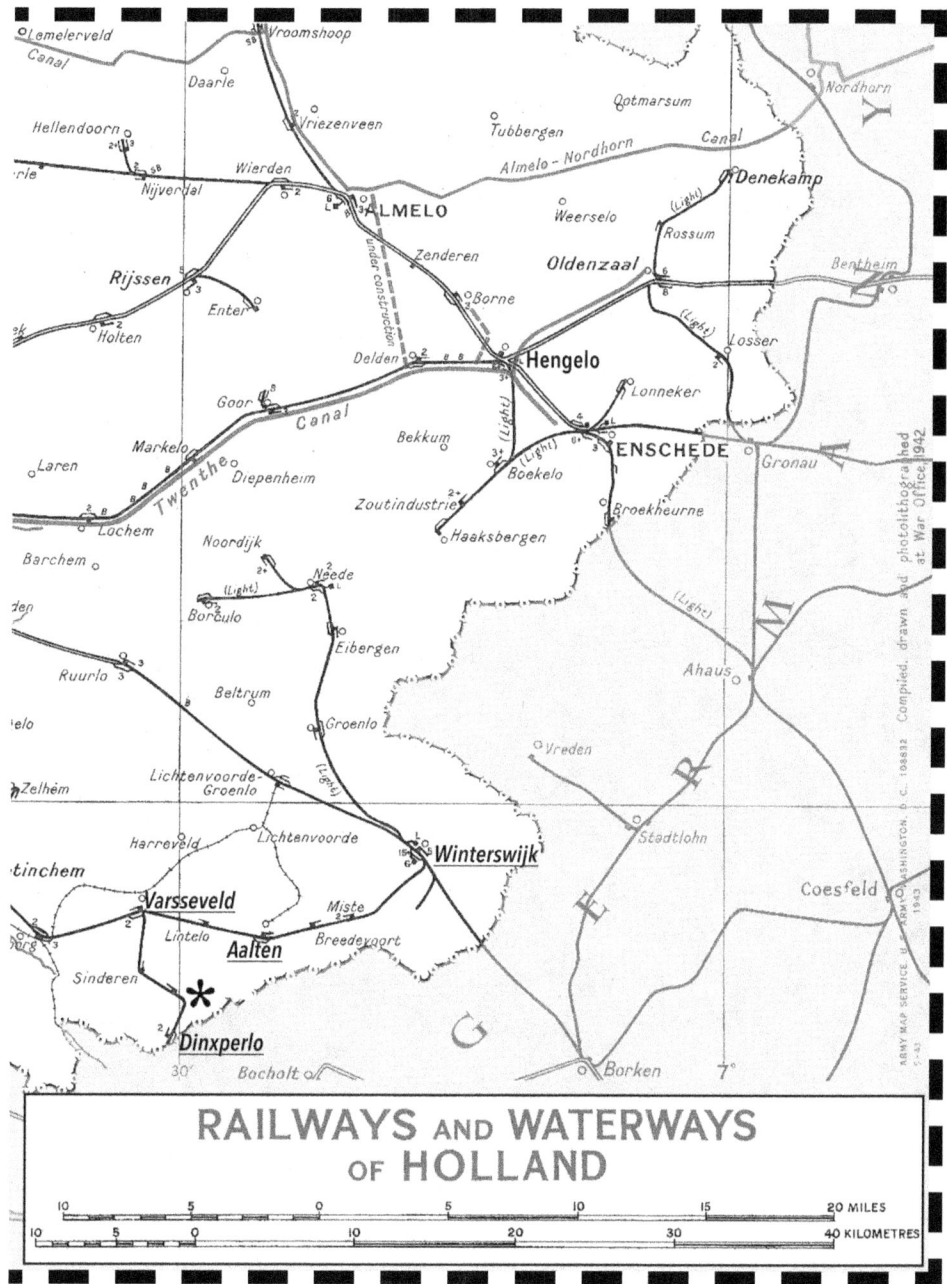

✶ = location of the Prinzen farm "Somsenhuis"

Courtesy of The Beinecke Rare Book and Manuscript Library, Yale University.
Adapted by Marc Seguin, 2020

Glossary

109: BF-109, the German single-engine fighter aircraft with a crew of one, also known as the Messerschmitt ME-109.

190: FW-190, the German single-engine fighter aircraft with a crew of one, known as the Focke-Wulf Würger (Shrike).

A-2 jacket: USAAF cotton-lined, leather flight jacket.

Ack-Ack guns: Anti-aircraft guns.

Alligator: A landing craft with tracks like a tank instead of wheels.

Arnhem: The Battle of Arnhem in September, 1944, was part of 'Operation Market Garden' during which Allied airborne troops were parachuted behind German lines in Holland to capture and hold a strategic bridge over the Lower Rhine River until the Allied tanks could reach them by road. The tanks were not able to break through, and many of the troops stranded at Arnhem were killed or captured by German forces.

B-15 jacket: USAAF wool-lined, leather flight jacket.

B-17: The American four-engine heavy bomber, known as the Flying Fortress, with a crew of nine or ten.

Bazooka: American hand-held, anti-tank rocket launcher.

BBC: British Broadcasting Corporation

Bren gun: British light machine gun, .303 calibre.

C-47: The American-made twin-engine transport aircraft, known as the Dakota, Skytrain and DC-3.

'Can Do' Bomb Group: The nickname given to the 305th Bombardment Group, one of more than 40 bombardment groups of the American 8th Air Force stationed in Britain between 1942 and 1945.

CeeBees: Also, Seabees or CB's — American Naval Construction Battalions.

Colt .45:   The standard American Army issue handgun, .45 calibre.

DH-98:   The British twin-engine fighter/bomber with a crew of two, known as the Mosquito.

Ersatz: Substitute for coffee, usually made from chicory.

Fieseler Storch (Stork):   Small, light German aircraft.

Flak: Anti-aircraft fire.

Flying Fortress: The American four-engine heavy bomber with a crew of ten, designated the B-17.

Focke-Wulf: See FW-190.

German jet fighter: The twin-engine Messerschmitt ME-262 aircraft with a crew of one was the world's first operational jet-powered fighter aircraft, known as the Schwalbe (Swallow).

Gestapo: The German Geheime Staatspolizei, the secret State police.

GI Bill: Also GI Bill of Rights — The U.S government's Servicemen's Readjustment Act of 1944.

K-rations: A food pack issued to American forces for consumption in the field.

Lancaster (Lanc):   The British and Commonwealth four-engine heavy bomber with a crew of seven.

Luftwaffe: The German air force.

Luger :   The standard German Army issue handgun, 9mm calibre.

Mae West: An inflatable life jacket worn by Allied aircrew.

Mauser: Standard German Army issue infantry rifle, 7.62mm calibre.

ME-262:   See German jet fighter.

Messerschmitt: See German jet fighter and BF-109.

Mosquito: See DH-98.

P-47: The American single-engine fighter aircraft with a crew of one, known as the Thunderbolt.

P-51: The American single-engine fighter aircraft with a crew of one, known as the Mustang.

RAAF: Royal Australian Air Force.

RAF: Britain's Royal Air Force.

RCAF: Royal Canadian Air Force.

'Second Dicky' trip: A new pilot's orientation flight during which he only observes while another pilot flies the plane.

Sten gun: A British submachine gun, 9mm calibre.

Sterling bomber: The British four-engine heavy bomber with a crew of seven.

Togglier: The crewman on a B-17, in lieu of a bombardier, who toggled the bomb-release switches when the leading aircraft dropped its bombs.

Typhoon: The British single-engine fighter/bomber with a crew of one.

USAAF: The United States Army Air Forces.

V-1: *Vergeltungswaffe 1* (Retribution Weapon 1). Unmanned, German jet-powered flying bomb, known as a buzz bomb or doodlebug.

V-2: *Vergeltungswaffe 2* (Retribution Weapon 2). Unmanned, German rocket-powered guided missile used largely against targets in Britain and Belgium.

VE Day: Victory in Europe Day, May 8, 1945. The official celebration of the end of the war in Europe.

Wellington: The British twin-engine medium bomber with a crew of six.

Wireless Operator: A radio operator.

Seven On A Mat

by
Doris Mayberry
with
Owen Mayberry

Dedication

*We would like to dedicate this story to the Prinzen family
particularly Papa and Moeder Prinzen.
They lived through very tense times and it is hard to understand
how they managed to go through the close calls and responsibility
that they did and still keep an undying faith in God.*

Doris and Owen Mayberry
1995

Bernard (Papa) and Dora (Moeder) Prinzen, c.1940

Preface

This is not a story of war, but a story of struggle for survival because of the war. It is really about faith, luck, courage, and love for one's fellow human beings. All the Dutch people at the heart of this story were courageous, bold, risk takers. Sometimes they prayed; sometimes they laughed — for they loved a good joke. Always they were caring people.

We would like to extend our gratitude to the Dutch Underground, especially to Commander Jan Ket (Black Jan) and his second-in-command Hendrick Van t'Lam (Long Henk). They were all courageous and caring people.

There are many names we would like to list at this time who risked much to see that the seven were brought safely to the Prinzen farm, Somsenhuis:

> Henk ten Have
> Toni and Herman Overmars
> Miss Bake and Miss Smolders
> Mr. Sontink
> Mr. and Mrs. Veenendahl
> Count S.J. Van Limburg Stirum
> Co Hettinga
> and many others whose names we do not have.

On behalf of the other six airmen, a few names we have are Mr. J.H. Harmsen, and the other brave and kind people who helped Chuck; all the unnamed people who helped Jim; the caring Dutchmen who first found Bob and the doctor and forest ranger (Henry) and others even including the doctor that treated Bob in the prison hospital, and all those unnamed who helped Frank and Joe; we thank you.

A special thanks to all those who willingly gave us their stories and permission to use them.

Preface

    I might add here that my information for this book came from tapes, personal interviews, books, and letters, as well as newspaper articles. Owen spent many hours at my elbow while I was putting this together. I needed his input very much not only because he was there, but because he understood the wordage that was needed to be used in so many instances. Unfortunately, fifty years is a long time, and he, understandably, had a problem remembering everything vividly. Some of what he does remember has faded through time.

    This book was written in memory of Dora and Bernard Prinzen who certainly must have earned their places in Heaven.
    Also in memory of Major Jan Ket of the Dutch Underground who took unaccountable chances for his country and seven airmen far from home.

Doris Mayberry
1995

Background

The Seven Allied Airmen

Francis (Frank) Dell was born in England, raised in the town of Brighton in southern England and received an excellent education. He joined the RAF early on, spent part of his time teaching cadets how to fly at a military base in the American South [Moody Field, Georgia]. With his personality, he became the unelected leader of the group. [RAF. DH-98 Mosquito pilot. Six months behind enemy lines.]

Joseph (Joe) Davis, believed to have been born in Florida, chose a military career and, before embarking overseas, had accumulated an impressive number of flying hours. A very intelligent man, he was sometimes impatient with those who were not quite so intelligent. He married before going to Europe during WWII. [USAAF. P-51 Mustang pilot. Six months behind enemy lines.]

Robert (Bobby) Brown was born and raised in northern California and spent most of his young life before the war in San Francisco. He joined the USAAF very enthusiastically and was eager to learn to fly and serve his country. [USAAF. P-51 Mustang pilot. Five months behind enemy lines.]

Owen Mayberry was born and raised in northern California on a ranch. Ever since he was a small boy watching birds in flight, he wanted to learn to fly. He took aircraft maintenance training in southern California, and subsequently obtained a position with the government in the Sacramento area. When the United States entered WWII, he was given a deferment, but later joined the USAAF and subsequently became co-pilot on a B-17. Owen was married before going overseas and the father of a

Background: The Seven Allied Airmen

baby girl — the only father in the group of airmen. The other "evadees" nicknamed him 'Pop'. [USAAF. B-17 Flying Fortress co-pilot. Four months behind enemy lines.]

Theodore (Ted) Roblee* came from Wisconsin. He lost his mother early in his life, so when he went into the service, he left a widowed father behind. After taking his training, he was subsequently included in a flight crew as togglier. He and Owen were on the same crew. The crew was commanded by Henry Schmidt from California. [USAAF. B-17 Flying Fortress sergeant/togglier. Four months behind enemy lines.]

James (Jim) Strickland from Australia, the son of a Protestant minister, took his training as an RAAF wireless operator in his own country and was further trained in England. He flew 26 missions over Europe before this story takes place. Jim was a vigorous and healthy young male, which was handy for walking one hundred miles out of Germany. [RAAF. Avro Lancaster sergeant/wireless operator. Seven weeks behind enemy lines.]

Charles (Chuck) Huntley was born in Plato, Saskatchewan, Canada. He became a pilot with the RCAF, flying a Lancaster when his part of this story begins. [RCAF. Avro Lancaster pilot. Five weeks behind enemy lines.]

On March 30, 1945, the seven men were liberated.

---

* In the original 1995 manuscript, the author used the alias "Todd Boles" instead of the airman's real name. For historical accuracy, Ted Roblee's real name has been used in this edition.

2nd Lt. Owen L. Mayberry, USAAF, 1944

Chapter 1

Owen's Story

It was November 26, 1944. I was flying my seventh mission as co-pilot of a B-17 bomber. We were about four hours out of England when we started our bomb run. The bomb bay doors opened on the lead ship. Ted Roblee, the togglier, opened our bomb bay doors and released our bombs at the same time as the lead ship, calling "Bombs Away" over the intercom.

As the B-17 lightened its load over the oil refineries at Misburg, Germany, I immediately adjusted the elevator trim tab to compensate for the 6,000 pound loss.

"Bomb bays clear!" called Tom Horger, the flight engineer.

"Bomb bays closing," Ted informed us.

"Let's get the Hell out of here!" The voice of Henry Schmidt, the commander, sounded relieved.

"What's going on, Hank? Look!" I pointed toward the rest of the 'Can Do' Bomb Group that appeared to be pulling up and away from us. Suddenly, there was a terrible high-pitched whine. The Flying Fortress began vibrating violently. Hank gripped the wheel hard.

"Number two engine's running away! Feather it!" he shouted. I hesitated. Everything was shaking so much. The instrument panel was a blur. Hank hit the feathering button, but number two didn't feather. I shut down the engine. Still the propeller continued to windmill.

"Number one's running away! Feather it!" Hank spoke through clenched teeth. His face was the color of pale green marble. I hit the feathering button and shut down the engine.

The windmilling stopped.

"There's a big hole under the forward part of the left wing," Leo reported, "and smaller holes all over. This baby's a sieve!"

"The flak got us!" Tom's voice came to them in a kind of muffled appeal over the intercom. A wave of helplessness flooded the cockpit and we savagely brushed it aside as Hank and I fought to keep the crippled bomber steady. Our intensive training took over automatically. We were responsible for nine lives.

"Steady everybody! Stay alert!" Hank's voice was calmer now, but his expression was still agitated.

A chill was spreading through the cabin since cabin heat came from the engines. I demanded and received an answer from each person every few minutes to make sure no man's oxygen mask froze. Now we had only the warmth from our electrical flying clothes.

Meanwhile, I began scraping ice that was forming on the inside of the windshield. I was so nervous and scared, the sweat ran down my arms from my hand and down my body from my armpits.

I adjusted the rudder controls to compensate for the loss of power on the port side. As I checked each man, I urged him to lighten the load. I ordered each man to dump everything not needed.

We all knew we could be picked off by enemy fighters. Fearfully, I looked at Hank just as the commander spoke into the intercom.

"Tom, fire the flare. We need fighter protection."

"Roger!" Tom quickly answered.

Terry Messing, the navigator, called for a heading toward London, "Until I can plot a more accurate course." His voice was all business.

"Roger, Terry." Hank turned the airplane and adjusted to emergency power trying to prevent loss of altitude.

Four P-47's with black and white checkered cowlings appeared above our struggling bomber. It was a beautiful sight to see. The P-47's criss-crossed back and forth above us for about ten minutes. As they veered off, four P-51's took over protection duties. In the distance, we could see the contrails of German jet fighters. They either didn't see us or were more interested in the bomber formations. This method of protection continued for about an hour and a half.

"We're going to make it," Hank muttered almost inaudibly.

During a periodic visual check of the starboard side, I saw oil coming out of the cowling of number four engine.

"Hank, number four is seeping oil and the temperature's rising." I felt almost calm now.

"Reduce power on number four," Hank ordered quietly. "I need whatever it can give us." His voice sounded calm too, but his face was pale and still slightly green under his light brown hair.

"Terry, better give me a heading for the Zuider Zee. We may have to ditch this thing." He spoke into the mouthpiece before him.

"Roger!"

"We've lost a lot of altitude," I said. "We are now at 17,000 feet and are losing 250 feet per minute."

"Yea, I know," Hank turned his head so that the words would not go into the intercom, "hope we can get to the Zuider Zee!"

About an hour later, we crossed the Dutch border. Suddenly, number two engine burst into flames. Hank immediately flipped the toggle switch and rang the bell three times.

"Prepare to bail out!" he called.

"We're awfully low, Hank," I warned. "Twelve hundred feet!"

Hank switched on the alarm. It rang steadily. The crew fastened on their chest packs.

"Bail out! Bail out!"

Keith Hereford, the tail gunner, Tom Lattimore, the waist gunner, Leo Weocyewski, the ball turret gunner, and Bob Willson, the radio operator, checked out as they left through the rear escape door.

"A pin is jammed on the forward hatch." Terry's voice over the intercom penetrated the urgency in the cockpit.

"Go see what you can do, Owen," the commander was manually assisting the auto-pilot to maintain control. He didn't even look at me.

"On my way." I moved to stand.

"Put on your 'chute, and bail out when you get the door released!"

"I've got to put on my shoes. I'm wearing my flight boots."

"There's no time! Hurry!" Hank barked, "When you get it open, don't wait! Bail out!"

I was already snapping my parachute to the harness in front of me. I quickly heaved myself from the co-pilot's seat and made my way to the front escape hatch. I found that one hinge pin would not release. I sat down opposite the hinge side. Then I kicked downward on the door with one foot and pushed the other foot down on the released pin side. That action twisted the door into the slipstream, which tore the door off and it fell to the field below.

I looked up at Terry, raised my right arm in a half salute and called "So-o-o long-g-g!"

Tom Horger, engineer; Ted Roblee, togglier; Terry Messing, navigator, and Hank Schmidt, the commander, were still in the plane when I left. As I dropped through the escape hatch, my right hand grasped the rip cord. Since I had my right arm in an up position, it caused me to do a half turn. I saw three blossomed 'chutes to the rear. When my parachute opened my neck got a nasty jolt and I felt nauseous. I almost blacked out. There was just time to notice that there was a farmhouse below, a fence, and a small grove of young trees. I tried to concentrate on relaxing my knees as I learned during training. I didn't notice the ditch until I was up to my waist in water. Water filled my boots, clothes, helmet, and goggles as it splashed high above my head.

I floundered around blindly as the parachute settled over me. I freed myself of it and finally crawled from the ditch. In a half-crouch position,

I removed my goggles and helmet, then dropped them on the wet ground. One end of the parachute caught on the barbed-wire fence. I yanked it free and managed to collapse it and roll it into a crude ball. I tucked it under my left arm, picked up my helmet and goggles and began to run, still half crouched, for the grove of trees about thirty yards away. My flight was like the slow motion of a dream because my boots were heavy with water. I made a sloshing sound with every step. My heart beat madly in my chest and I was gasping for breath.

Finally, in the dubious protection of the trees, I found a hole by some tree roots. There, I hastily removed and buried my Mae West and the parachute, and stuffed my helmet and goggles into my jacket pocket. I sat on the ground, emptied my boots and put them back on, then stood upright for the first time since I landed. I looked around in the semi-darkness of the forest for a place to hide. Not far away I saw another hole in the ground by a tree. I hurried to it and folded my long frame in half as I squeezed myself backwards into the hole.

My feet and ankles were exposed so I broke off the branch of a young fir tree within reach and stuck the broken end into the ground to hide my size twelves. By ducking my head a little, I could see out through the lacy, green of the little branch.

A small crowd of farmers who had no doubt seen the smoking plane and the billowing parachutes gathered together. They were nearby, talking quietly but excitedly among themselves. Occasionally, one of them would point or look in my direction.

'Why don't they go away! They'll give me away!' I thought. I could hear the motor and clacking sound of a half-track truck approaching and the voices of the soldiers who were undoubtedly looking for the crew of the doomed bomber. My nerves were jumping now. I tried to double up even more in the cold, damp hole in hopes of making myself smaller, without success.

A man came, knelt down and spoke. "I am Henk. Do you speak English?"

"Yes," I answered, "where am I?"

"In East Holland, near Wesepe and very close to my farm."

"Where is the front?"

"About fifty kilometers."

"Oh, I can walk that distance in two days!"

"You cannot walk there by yourself. It is not safe. You must stay hidden until the night comes. They are looking for you now."

"Where's the rest of my crew?"

"I do not know, but I will try to find out."

"Can you make those people go away?" I asked gesturing toward the group of curious farmers.

Henk rose immediately and walked over to them. He spoke first to a boy of about fifteen who nodded and moved back toward me. Meanwhile Henk quietly persuaded the three others to leave, leading them off himself into the grove of trees where they quickly disappeared from sight.

The boy squatted down and, without speaking, pointed to a broken pocket watch in his hand. It had no crystal and only an hour hand. He moved the hand to six, then pointed to the pale winter sun and with outstretched arm, moved his pointing finger down to the West.

After that, he spread the fingers of both hands, palms downward and gestured toward the ground, then put a forefinger across his lips. I nodded. Someone would be back at six o'clock. I was to stay hidden and quiet. I needed no encouragement.

The boy moved away quickly and silently disappeared into the grove of trees in the same direction as the rest.

Owen's Rescue

I guessed I had about three hours to wait so I burrowed as far as I could into the hole and shivered as I listened to the sound of the half-track. Its motor faded and grew stronger in turns as the systematic search continued. When the vehicle was within sight, I saw it stop and several soldiers got out with bicycles. I was certain I would be found, but they rode down the road toward an open field. They did not return to where I was hiding. It seemed like an eternity passed, and finally the motor sounds got farther and farther away. I began to relax. I felt so tired! In spite of the cold ground and chilly air, I even dozed a little.

Later, when a low ground mist hid half the setting sun, I checked my watch. It was five o'clock. There was no sound except for a couple of birds announcing the end of the day. 'Time to move,' I thought, remembering my survival training: Do not trust anyone completely who offers to help. I crawled out of the hole, stood up, and stretched full length. I bent to brush the dirt from my clothes and looked around for another place to wait. I walked deeper into the grove of trees, sat on the ground and leaned against one of the larger trees. I could see my former hiding place.

'Well, here you are, you prune-picker farm boy! What happens now?' I was happy to be alive. Somehow, I could not muster up any amount of worry about my situation. Light from a full moon filtered into the grove. I was day dreaming about home. Nearly daylight there, I guessed. What was the day? Saturday, I think. How are my wife and baby? Snug and safe and probably asleep, I hope. My wife is going to wonder why no more letters pretty soon now and begin to worry. I sighed. Well, that can't be helped. Suddenly, I heard muffled footsteps and a faint whistle. I quickly rose to my feet and moved closer. There was a man standing in the moonlight. He was looking around near the hiding place where I had been, then signaled with another low whistle. Finally, I decided to take a chance and walked up to him. Then I realized this person was not Henk who had spoken to me before. He was older and shorter and about twenty-five years old. I felt uncertain.

"Call me Ben," the stranger spoke quietly with a heavy accent. We shook hands. "It is not my name, of course." He took out a pouch of tobacco and paper and began to roll a cigarette.

"You want a cigarette?" he asked, and I shook my head and watched him closely. "We must wait until it is darker. We'll talk a few minutes and then I will take you to a farmer's home down the road."

Ben sat on a mound of earth and leaned against a tree. I sat on the ground, resting my arms on my knees. While I listened to the dark-haired Dutchman talk about the war, I watched his face steadily, answering his questions only briefly.

"Where is Henk, who was here before?" I finally broke in, and Ben shrugged.

"He lost his nerve. He is very young, you see. He can speak English

Owen's Story

very well and the people in the village know this. Some of them are not his good friends so I came because I am not from here." Ben exhaled a cloud of smoke.

"Are you hurt?" he asked. "Do you need a doctor?"

"No. Only my clothes are wet from landing in the water."

Suddenly an ear-splitting roar wracked the silence of the night. Terrified, I jumped to my feet. My companion was on his feet, too, muttering in Dutch.

"What was that?!" I gasped.

"A German rocket, launched toward Belgium," Ben said as he touched me on the wrist. I released my breath. I remembered hearing about the V-2 rocket Hitler boasted would end the war. Again, we sat on the ground.

"You have a wristwatch?" It was more a statement than a question.

"It's about fifteen minutes after six."

"Give it to me as I need it more than you will."

Startled, I hesitated, then shrugged and removed the watch. As I handed it to Ben, I thought, 'What the hell! I'll be back in England in a few days.' Ben quickly put the watch on his own wrist, and stood. He bent down and picked up a gunny sack.

"Here are civilian garments to cover your uniform." He tossed the bundle to me. "Put them on. It is time to go."

After struggling to get them on over my flight clothes, I hurried after Ben who had already started off down the pathway. With long strides I quickly caught up with my guide. Ben, dressed in dark clothing, was difficult to see in the shadows of the moonlit trees. Before long, we walked out of the grove and reached a road where there were two bicycles beneath the bushes.

"You can ride a bicycle?" Ben asked.

"Yes," I answered, feeling a little annoyed when Ben seemed surprised.

Ben grunted and climbed on a bicycle and led the way. I followed close behind. Every few minutes we stopped. Ben rode alone down the road to see if the way was clear. When he returned, we continued.

About 30 minutes later, he turned to the right into a driveway, rode around in back of the house, got off the bicycle and leaned it against a tree. I did the same. Ben knocked on a back door. The door opened and a man stood silhouetted in the light of the doorway. They spoke to each other softly in Dutch.

"I am Herman." He introduced himself to me and we shook hands. I immediately felt friendship for this big blonde Dutchman.

"Come, we will climb up the ladder to the upstairs bedroom. My family must not see you in case questions are asked later." He stepped outside, closing the door behind him and led the way along the back of the house. He climbed the ladder and opened a small door then turned and beckoned to us to follow.

I climbed the ladder and entered a bedroom. Ben came in behind me.

"Take off your wet clothes and lie down on the bed," Herman said, "We will dry them for you." I obediently removed my clothes and lay on the bed. Ben covered me with a quilt. Herman gathered up the wet clothes and left the room through a door to the hallway.

I stretched my tired body on the bed. 'Oh Boy! A comfortable place to sleep tonight!' I thought.

Herman soon returned with mugs of ersatz and a plate of sandwiches on a tray. He set the tray on a low chest of drawers near the bed, smiled at me, and left the room again.

When I took a bite of my sandwich and found it was raw bacon, I could not swallow it.

"I'm sorry," I apologized to Ben. "I'm not used to eating uncooked bacon."

Ben nodded. He took the sandwich, slipped the bacon out, added it to his own, then handed back the bread and butter. Gratefully, I ate the bread. Ben munched his sandwich and grinned at me.

"There are many things I wish to learn. I have never met an American before. What is it like to jump from an airplane? Were you frightened?" I answered all the questions without hesitation this time.

"Where are you from? Are you from a farm?"

"I grew up on a prune ranch in Northern California."

"Are you married? Do you have children?"

"I have a wife and baby girl at home." There were many questions, and I would have preferred to spend that time sleeping. After nearly an hour the door opened. Herman came in bringing back the clothes and carrying a pair of leather shoes. He laid them all on a nearby chair and walked to the door again. There he paused and turned to me.

"I will not see you again. Ben will look after you. He will take you to the next place."

Before I could answer, the door closed quietly behind him.

"Dress, please," Ben began handing me my clothes. "Here are shoes. Your boots tell too much. The shoes are better."

Reluctantly I dressed. I put on my officer pinks [the winter service uniform] and covered them with the civilian clothes. The hand-made shoes were too small, but I finally got them on my feet. I left my electric flying suit, boots and B-15 jacket on the chair, took one longing look at the warm comfortable bed, and followed my guide down the ladder.

Ben took off at right angles to the back door of Herman's house. We tramped across a plowed field and I could smell the damp soil and manure. Ben stopped to relieve himself once. I decided that was a good idea. Then I followed the moonlit figure for about fifteen minutes more. The moon shining on the thick ground mist diffused the light and Ben's dark figure was difficult to see. The tight shoes soon caused pain in both feet. I wondered how much farther, when we reached a small, forlorn-looking hut. The roof line had a crooked sway-backed look and reminded me of an old mare that was pastured across the road from our ranch. The thatch needed replacing.

"Here," Ben spoke, and rapped lightly on the door. The door opened almost immediately. "This is Pete," Ben said and introduced me to Pete in Dutch.

Pete thrust out his rough work-worn hand. His long thin face broke into a smile and he gestured us into the little room. There was bread and cheese on the table. Pete poured cups of tea. We all sat. Ben and Pete exchanged some words, but Pete wasn't much of a talker. After a while, Ben got up from the table and disappeared through a brick opening in the back wall. He stuck his head back through the opening and beckoned to me.

"Come! We will sleep here," he said. I stooped down and entered a little alcove. A thick layer of straw covered the floor. Ben lay down and covered himself completely with straw. He was asleep almost at once. I lay down and covered myself as well as I could. I made the whole trip from England over again in my mind, reliving every move, every word, every gesture.

Finally, I fell asleep.

"Ah! You are awake now." I saw Ben seated at the table when I crawled out of the brick opening. "It is nearly midday. It is good that you rested." He inclined his head toward a door in the north wall, "To the water closet," he added.

Later, we sat around the table and talked. Ben interpreted between Pete and me. As the hours of waiting for sundown went by, I began to learn a little Dutch. The most important words I learned were; '*ja*' for yes, and '*danka*' for thank you. I found many reasons to say '*danka*'.

Chapter 2

Ted

Late in the afternoon, there was a knock on the door. When Pete opened it, I could see a young man. He talked briefly to Pete in Dutch. Pete opened the door wider and he stepped inside.

'He looks familiar. Where have I seen him before?' I thought. He walked over to me and sat down at the table.

"I am Henk, remember?" I smiled and nodded. We shook hands.

"You were there when I landed in the ditch yesterday. You made the people go away," I said.

Henk nodded, "I have news for you. We have found one of your crew."

I felt relieved.

"Great! Who is it?"

"He gives his name as Ted Roblee. He is your togglier?"

"Yes. Is he OK?" Henk nodded. "Not hurt?"

"He is fine." He grinned at the pleasure on my face. "We have him lodged in another place where you will go tonight. You will stay at the home of two maiden ladies." He added with a twinkle, "in their sixties."

"Yes," Ben broke in, "you two will stay there until it is clear to move you again. It is not wise to stay in one place too long."

"Also," Henk continued, "I went into the village this afternoon. I saw the rest of your crew. They had the same sign on their shoulders you have." I felt apprehensive.

"Yes, they are prisoners. They were put into a building across from the school house. I am sorry."

I looked down at my hands. "At least they are all alive." The words 'for now' were not spoken.

There was quiet in the room, then Ben stood.

"Time to go." I stood up too, and turned to Henk grasping his hand in both of mine.

"*Danka.* I have learned a word today. I'll never be able to thank you — everyone — enough."

"We will see each other again before you leave the area," Henk promised.

"I hope so," I replied and raised my hand in goodbye and moved to follow Ben out the door. As before, we walked across plowed fields and through grassy meadows. The pungent smell of manure, earth and dampness was strong in the air as I concentrated on keeping up with my guide's figure showing dimly in the ground mist.

Very soon, we could see the outlines of a big broad house surrounded by bushes that looked like black cotton in the darkness. We skirted around an area of bushes to a door. Ben rapped softly.

A small, frail-looking, white-haired woman slowly opened the door. She peeked around it cautiously. Ben spoke to her and she opened it wider as she called to someone behind her. Ben turned to me and said, "This lady is Miss Bake, a retired school teacher." I inclined my head and murmured, "Ma'am."

"Come in! Come in! Tea is nearly ready. We've been expecting you." Miss Bake said in perfect English. Another woman, no taller, slightly older, and a little heavier stood behind her. "This is Miss Smolders who is staying here with me. She speaks no English."

Miss Smolders held out her hand to me. I took it, careful not to crush her fingers.

"I am leaving now," Ben said. "You are in good hands."

"Thanks for everything," I answered feeling slightly less enthusiastic than I had with the others. Ben raised his right arm in goodbye revealing his newly acquired wristwatch. I turned and followed the ladies into the kitchen.

Sitting at the table were two men. One was ruddy-faced with an expansive waistline. He wore the uniform of the local constabulary. The other had light hair and when he looked at me, I saw it was Ted. He jumped up excitedly. His tall, wiry frame almost catapulted from the chair that would have crashed over backwards but for the wall behind him. We slapped each other on the shoulders, sort of dancing around in our excitement. Both of us talked at once, laughing together.

"Hey, sit down! Sit down! I want you to meet the fellow who rescued me and brought me here. This is Constable Hans de Brink. Hans, this big guy was the co-pilot on our B-17." We greeted each other.

"Have you seen any of the others?" Ted asked anxiously.

"They're prisoners." Ted's happy expression sobered. The ladies set out tea. We all sat around the kitchen table and talked about the war and some of the incidents that happened locally. Then the constable rose from his chair.

"Are you leaving?" Ted's brown eyes looked up at him.

"I must, my friend. It is nearly curfew." Ted unabashedly rose and hugged the portly figure.

"There is no way to express my gratitude, Hans. Will we ever meet again?"

"Perhaps, some day." Hans gently disengaged himself from the younger man's embrace, said his goodbyes to the ladies and me. Miss Bake accompanied him to the door. As he reached the kitchen door, he turned and waved.

"Take care of yourself," Ted responded, and Hans left the room.

Miss Smolders began washing up, and Miss Bake sat down at the table with us.

"I will show you where you are to sleep while you are here with us. First, two things I must warn you about. You must always stay together — all the time — so that if an emergency comes, we only have to look in one place to warn you. This saves a great deal of time. The other, is that you must not go outside or be near the outside door when someone knocks. We cannot hesitate very long in opening the door." Both of us nodded in understanding.

Miss Bake stood. "Come, I will show you your quarters. One of us will knock on your door in the morning when breakfast is ready. We eat early, around six so that everything is cleared away before most people are moving about." She led them up the stairway as she talked. The treads were wide enough so that her tiny feet needed a little extra step before she lifted her foot to the next step.

"There are two rooms upstairs separated by a bathroom. Miss Smolders sleeps downstairs so right now both rooms are empty." As she finished talking, she came to a door at the end of the hall. She opened the door. The room contained two cots separated by a small stand tucked beneath a tall narrow window. It was the only window in the room. She opened a door to the left revealing a small bathroom containing only a shower and a wash basin. Another door farther along the same wall led to the water closet.

"You must always prepare your room in the morning as though no one was occupying it. Everything must look neat and unused, if possible." When Miss Bake left the room, Ted and I talked very little while we prepared for bed.

My mind was in a whirl. It had been such an eventful two days. It surprised me when I heard a soft rapping on the door to call us to breakfast. Ted, already dressed, was making his bed.

That night there was a loud knock on the outside door. Ted and I scrambled quickly away from the kitchen table and headed for the stairs while Miss Smolders whisked the cups and plates off into a pan and deposited them in a cupboard. Miss Bake answered the door.

Later when Miss Bake knocked on our bedroom door, Ted moved to answer it. Both ladies were standing there.

"We've been told to leave our home tomorrow from eight in the morning until five in the evening." Miss Bake said. "The German army plans exercises in this area and they will be firing artillery. It would be dangerous for us to stay."

"What do we do?" Ted asked anxiously.

"The only thing left to do is hide beneath the house. Come, I will show you." She led the way down the staircase. On the third step from the bottom, she stopped and waited for us to pass her. We stopped and turned. Miss Bake bent over the fourth step. She moved the tread toward herself. Its movement on the riser was smooth and silent. We watched in admiration and surprise.

"Boy, that's neat!" Ted exclaimed.

"The sliding step was built purposely to hide food from the Germans," she said, "It also gives people like you a safe place to hide."

"We will give you enough food and water and a blanket to lie on under there. That is where you must spend the day tomorrow. We will call from here when we return. Here is a torch," she motioned to a flashlight lying on the top step.

Very early next morning both ladies were dressed to go out. Miss Bake held a basket of food and water. Miss Smolders carried a blanket over her arm. They handed both items to us then waited at the stairway until Ted and I were clear. We turned and looked up as the step slid back into place. Miss Bake's face was visible for a time.

She looked at us and said, "God be with you!" Then it was dark.

I turned on the flashlight and moved it around. In a crawling position we explored the area. There was not much space, but there was adequate room for the two of us.

We found a place to settle, spread the blanket and sat down, putting the food basket and water between us. I turned off the flashlight. Very dim light coming through the four vents, one on each four sides of the house, was the only indication that it was almost day time.

Except for our own breathing, there was no sound. The smell of soil and dust was our only indication of where we were. For some time we waited. I moved my position once to ease the numbness creeping up my legs. Ted cracked his knuckles nervously and heaved a sigh now and then.

Chapter 3

Ted's Story

Suddenly, there were booming noises, then silence, then several loud rumbles, then silence. For what seemed an eternity, the roar and rattle continued. The house sometimes shivered and settled. Once, when we heard glass shattering, Ted remarked, "I think the ladies just lost a window."

"I don't know why we are whispering, do you?" I asked quietly.

Ted giggled nervously, "Kind of silly, isn't it?"

"Ted, I never did ask you exactly what happened from the time you bailed out until you reached here. Tell me. It will make the time go faster."

. . .

O.K. Well, when I bailed out, I landed in an open grassy field. A pasture for animals, I guess. Not too big, and rectangular in shape. Nearby was a little house with some out buildings. I headed for the nearest one. It was a chicken house. I went in there to hide and maybe try to form some kind of a plan for when it got dark. Well, there were a few chickens in there — not many — maybe a dozen. Anyway, they raised a terrible racket. Boy! I was scared! I crouched down in the corner behind the nesting boxes and pretty soon the door opened and a pretty blue-eyed blonde girl about fifteen opened the door and stuck her head in.

"Come out." she called softly. "I know you are in there. I saw you come down in your parachute. The chickens also told me." She spoke in correct school book English.

"Come!" she repeated. "I will take you to a better hiding place. The chickens will be noisy every time you move!"

I stood up and followed her out the door.

"Where is your parachute?" she asked as she led me to another larger building.

Ted's Story

"I buried it out there," I told her as I pointed to a clump of bushes in the pasture.

"Good," she nodded, "I will pick it up after dark. Moeder will make clothes out of it."

"Be my guest," I answered. She opened the door to the little barn and the smell of pigs nearly knocked me down. But the pigs were penned at one end and at the other there was clean straw. Thick stacks of it. I stayed there all afternoon. I got used to the smell after awhile and didn't notice it.

When it was nearly dark, the girl came back and brought me some sandwiches and hot tea.

· · · · ·

"Raw bacon sandwiches?" I asked.

"Yea, how did you know?"

"I know! It was explained to me that cooking it made it shrink too much. Did you eat the raw bacon?"

"At first I had trouble. My stomach wanted to throw it back, but God, I was hungry! So I ate it anyway — and it stayed down somehow! I washed it down with hot tea and that helped."

"You did better than I did, Ted. What happened then?"

"The girl said I would have to stay there until about three or four in the morning and to get some sleep. She said if I covered myself with straw I'd have a better chance of keeping warm. After she left with the food tray, I settled down and actually slept for awhile. When the door opened again it was Hans — you met him here — he led me to this house before it was light, then he went off to work. He came back after work and that's how he was here when you came."

"Quite a bunch of people, these Dutch, aren't they?"

"How about you? What happened?"

I told him my story — even to losing my wristwatch.

When finally the booming stopped, Ted and I picked up everything and waited for the call from the ladies to go back upstairs.

That evening Henk returned. "You will be moved tomorrow morning before it is light — about four o'clock. Do you have watches?"

"Ted has," I answered "But Ben has mine."

"Why?"

"He said he needed it more than I did, and asked me for it, so I gave it to him."

Henk moved to the door. "I'll be back later." Then he left. I looked at Ted who was staring at the door.

"Who was that?" Ted asked. I explained.

"Where's he going?"

"Good question! I don't know. Maybe he'll tell us when he comes back."

After eight-o'clock curfew, there was a furtive knock on the door. Miss Bake opened it. Henk came in and he seemed upset.

"I went to see if I could find Ben." He said, "He wasn't supposed to take your watch. He is not from here and as far as I can find out he has left the area. I'm sorry. I hoped I could get your watch back."

"It's OK," I told him. "I'll get along."

"But it is not right. It gives the rest of us a bad name."

I shrugged.

"Anyway," Henk continued, "Your next guide will be Mr. Sontink. He will be here to guide you four days from now at five o'clock in the morning."

For the next four days, we busied ourselves with reading some of the books Miss Bake had on her shelves. I thoroughly enjoyed reading The Good Earth. We knew we were leaving very early the next morning, so Ted and I went to bed earlier than usual.

It was the morning of December 1st. Miss Bake was still in bed when we bid her goodbye. Miss Smolders was in the kitchen and had already given us each a hot cup of tea. We both gave each of the two ladies hugs and kisses knowing we would probably never see them again. Then we turned to follow Mr. Sontink who led us to his farm about a mile and half down the road. Since he spoke no English, we followed him silently.

We could see him in the moonlight so we kept him in sight all the time. It was a brisk walk. When finally we came to his farm, he took us into the kitchen and gave us a hot cup of ersatz and potato pancakes. They were very good.

Ted's Story

Mr. Sontink lived alone and a neighbor lady, Mrs. Overmars, wife of Herman, and the same lady who had dried my clothes, came to do cooking and housework and take care of things for him. After breakfast, he led us out into the barn part of the building and up a ladder into the hay where we stayed another four or five days.

While we were there, we would come downstairs in the evening for an hour or two. That first evening, we met members of a Jewish family who were also hiding from the Germans. The husband could speak English very well.

Mr. Sontink found a map of the United States and unfolded it on the table, and we pointed to where our homes were located. Ted found Milwaukee, Wisconsin, for them and I pointed out the approximate area of Sacramento, California, near where my home town village was located. Sacramento, I told them, is not far from San Francisco. I figured everyone had heard of San Francisco. We had a lively and interesting conversation for about an hour and a half, and then the farmer indicated it was time we went upstairs to our hiding place. These friendly conversations went on each evening in Mr. Sontink's front parlor.

During the daytime, while hiding in the hay mow in the barn, we could see through a small round window. Sometimes we saw German V-2 Vengeance Bombs, as Hitler called them, or we saw the contrails when they were fired. We could hear the sound of the firing in the distance just like the evening of the day we parachuted. We also heard many of the V-1's, or buzz bombs, that had their own frightening sound. I counted as many as twenty-seven in one day. We felt lucky none came down near us.

Our next move was in the middle of the night. We left Mr. Sontink's house and went to a castle. This man, whom we knew only as Mr. Veenendahl, was chauffeur for the estate. He took us to his residence where his wife had the customary tea, or ersatz coffee, and some sort of sweet they had acquired. We did not ask where they got it.

We spent four or five days with the Veenendahl family. Germans were billeted in the Castle Hoenlo where there was also a contingent of Dutch workers forced into labor for the Third Reich. We stayed upstairs in the chauffeur's house. Mr. Veenendahl was one of the chess champions of

Holland. He wanted us to play. I didn't play, but Ted knew a little about it. He tried to play, but Mr. Veenendahl was very skilled.

This was our last stay in the area of Olst.

One night a gentleman came to the house. He spoke excellent English. He told us his name was Sam Stirum and he would be our leader for our next move in the early morning.

We would travel for a distance of fifty or sixty miles. The area where we were to go was just outside Aalten and very near the Dutch/German border. This man was a fascinating personality. He wore riding breeches, slip-in leather black boots, a tan sport coat, and a derby hat very much like hats worn during a fox hunt. He was about five feet eight inches tall, wore a mustache and had a high-pitched, staccato speech. He told us we would be riding bicycles, and he would lead us about half-way. We would then stay near Zutphen overnight. Two fellows of the Dutch Underground would then lead us the rest of the way to our destination.

Chapter 4

The Farm Somsenhuis

Very early next morning after breakfast, Ted and I gathered our belongings, said goodbye to Mr. and Mrs. Veenendahl, thanked them for taking such risks for us, and then there was a knock on the door. Mr. Veenendahl opened it and Mr. Stirum greeted us.

"Good morning, men. Good morning, Mr. and Mrs. Veenendahl." Then to us, "I see you are ready to travel."

"Yes, we are ready," Ted answered.

"I hope you can ride bicycles. It is quite a distance." Again, I felt an annoyance. 'They must think in this country that Americans are born driving a car,' I thought. I had a chance to regret that thought. I didn't tell him it had been about five years since I was on a bike, so probably wasn't in very good shape anyway.

"Best we begin our journey," he said. We followed him out the door and got on bicycles that were provided for us.

"I will ride seventy-five to one hundred feet ahead of you at all times," our guide told us. "There is a reason for this. If I am stopped by German soldiers, you would have a chance to go back or turn off the road. If you were stopped and I wasn't, I could go on, avoiding capture."

So we began our journey down the road.

After about an hour and half, the sky began to get light. We stopped occasionally, got off our bicycles to rest before continuing. By this time, I began to think, 'Wow! I'm not at all sure I can make it.'

We began to see dim lights in the houses we passed. About eight-thirty we saw in the distance a formation of German soldiers coming down the road. A knot of fear began forming in my stomach. I don't know how Ted felt, but I suspect it wasn't much different.

Before we got close to them, our guide called back to us, "Just go on like you are a worker. Pay no attention to them. Keep on riding," he said.

"They probably won't even bother you."

We soon approached them close enough so that we could hear them singing in cadence. Some of them said, "Good morning," in German. We just grunted a greeting and that was that.

As we continued on, we passed a single soldier, wearing a black uniform of the Home Guard. He had a Luger in a holster at his waist in the back as they all did. The Home Guard consisted of older men. I found out later that their duties were to observe and maintain community order.

"Good morning," he greeted us in German as we rode past.

Then we came to a canal. A bridge crossed this canal. There was a German soldier on the bridge. Mr. Stirum motioned us off the road where we waited under cover of some bushes until the soldier moved off the bridge.

Finally, he walked on by and we got back on the road and continued our journey. We weren't taking chances. He might have been there to check every one's identification. We had fake papers and might have gotten by, but we did not want the risk.

We had several incidents like that. Either German soldiers or Dutch workers were being marched down the road by Germans to their assigned work details for the day.

We reached the halfway point where we were to rest up for the night. We went into this house and the woman of the house and Mr. Stirum spoke in Dutch. Then he turned to Ted and me.

"You cannot stay here," he said, "The Germans were suspicious and raided this house yesterday." However, she gave us food and hot liquids to drink. Very soon our new guides came to the house to take us the rest of the way. We shook hands with Mr. Stirum and thanked him for his help.

As we were riding down the road, we met German soldiers many times. Each time, they greeted us, apparently suspecting nothing. During one of our rest stops in mid-afternoon when we stopped for a snack along the trail, one of our two guides, Co Hettinga, asked us, "Did you know that man who was your guide is a Count?"

"I sure didn't," I answered.

"A Count? Gee!" Ted issued a low whistle.

"Yes, he is Graaf S.J. Van Limburg Stirum. He is from a very prominent Dutch family. His brother was killed during the Holland invasion."

"Is that what 'Graaf' means? Count?" Ted asked.

"Yes," he answered, smiling at our astonishment.

We got back on our bicycles and continued. Once, when we passed by a little house, we saw a German officer standing outside beside his bicycle pulling on his gloves. He watched us all the time we were passing. "Oh, Boy!" I thought, "He suspects us of being the enemy." I fully expected him to draw his gun and shout, "Halt!"

Ted said he felt the same way. However, the German officer was apparently on his way to his official duties and he didn't bother us. We were pretty tense just the same.

By late afternoon, we began to reach the farm that was our destination. My legs were beginning to tire. The last mile or two I could no longer make my legs go around. They just would not pedal any more. Ted apparently had no trouble, probably because he was three or four years younger than I. One of the leaders, Hans, a very husky fellow with legs of tremendous power, took hold of the handlebars of my bike and powered it as well as his. He pulled me into a shed of the farm where we headed. Ted made it all the way under his own power.

When we got into the shed, I couldn't even get off the bicycle except by falling to the floor. My legs felt numb. We rested for a few minutes until I could get on my feet. Then we followed our guide across the yard and through a door. They didn't have to knock, so we were expected. We later found that it was the custom to walk in without knocking. I had a little trouble with that.

We passed through the barn part of the building, through the dell and into the residence section of the Prinzen farm, Somsenhuis.

To our surprise, there were three other Allied flyers with the Dutch family. We were introduced all around: Lt.* Francis H. Dell, RAF, (Frank), Lt. Joseph Davis, USAAF (Joe), and Lt. Robert Brown, USAAF (Bob or Bobby), Bernard Prinzen (Papa) and his wife, Dora (Moeder)

---

* Lt = Lieutenant, the commissioned officer rank below Captain, pronounced "leftenant" in the British and Commonwealth forces and "lootenant" in the American forces.

and their ten children. There were six boys: Hendrick, Jan, Derk, Willum, Marinus, and little Benny. There were also four girls: Truida, Hermein, Johanna and Anna.

Then Bob spoke, "Well, Frank, you thought surely these guys would be English flyers." So I guess Frank was sort of disappointed. A little homesick, I imagine.

The oldest daughter set food before us and our guides said their good-byes and left. The date was December 9. It had been thirteen days since Ted and I had parachuted out of our B-17.

After that long bicycle trip, the tension, and the other bicycle trips, we were two very tired flyers. Frank, Joe and Bob showed us the hiding place where we were to sleep in the hay above the pump room.

When we climbed the ladder, Frank was carrying a carbide light to light our way. They pointed out the small room that was a space cleared in the hay. The cleared area was approximately eight by fourteen feet and not high enough for Bob to stand up to his full five feet six inches. At one end of the room were various weapons — guns, ammunition, hand grenades, and other defensive items. There was about six by eight feet left for five or six of us to sleep. There was a generous thickness of straw over the floor. On top of the straw lay a quilt for more cushioning and comfort and extra blankets for warmth.

"You've come a great distance today and you both must be very tired. We'll leave you so you two can rest. We will show you around later when you come down and it's safer to go outside for a little while," said Frank.

Gratefully, Ted and I bedded down in that little room. We were both soon asleep.

Later, when we came down the ladder, our fellow escapees were in the dell talking and kidding with Truida, the oldest girl. They asked us to join them. I set the carbide light down on a board.

"Tell me, Frank, is this the kind of lighting this farm has everywhere?"

"Yes," he answered, "You see, there is no electricity here on this farm, no natural gas, the heat comes from wood, the lights are carbide lights. Just a little can that has a top to it. Carbide powder and a little water are mixed together in a can and that creates fumes. You light it and it makes a little light, more light than a candle, but not as much as an electric light. There is one kerosene lamp the family uses once or twice, but kerosene

The Farm Somsenhuis

is quite scarce. Most of the time carbide lights are used. You'll notice that when the lid is put back on, the light goes out."

"How about telling us about the guns and ammo that are there in the hayloft," Ted asked.

"Yea, those are the guns we have cleaned or still need cleaning," Bob explained. "And we have to clean off the cosmoline anyway, but when the guns land barrel end in the mud, then we have an extra job. You will want to help us, no doubt, but not today. The day is nearly over and we want to show you the Prinzen farm."

Ted and I followed them outside and in the light of what was left of the day, they pointed out what we could see without going too far from the door.

This farm, called Somsenhuis, was about fifteen acres with a dirt road leading to a bigger main thoroughfare. The dirt road was about 900 feet long. The farm had some out buildings for tools and another for wood cutting and storage. There were some hay stacks, and there were pits dug and filled with sand and sawdust. These pits were dug in the summer for storing vegetables to feed the animals and for the family's table during the winter. Under one of the hay stacks by the road, a hole had been prepared where guns were hidden.

One day there was a warning that the Germans were coming. Many times, this warning came from the youngest child, Benny, who came running in the house calling loudly, *"Komen ze mufs,"* or something that sounded like that. It was his word for Germans. We slipped out to our hiding place.

Afterwards, Frank, who could understand some Dutch, told us that those Germans were there to search the grounds. They moved every board they saw under that hay stack where guns were stashed, but failed to move the very board that would have revealed the guns. Frank understood a little more Dutch than I since he had been at the farm two or three months longer. He knew French quite well, however. He had the opportunity to practice his French when two French Resistance members would show up at the farm or wherever Frank was at the time.

The following days, the five of us cleaned guns, making sure no indication of the cleaning process was out in the open. Everything was done in the little room, with ammo and guns stored at one end of the room.

Somsenhuis 1944 - 45, by Owen Mayberry

That left us a space at the other end near a brick wall for sleeping. There were hundreds and hundreds of rounds of 9mm ammunition which would fit certain Luger pistols as well as British Sten guns. We had a good supply of both, plus various pistols and gas-charged Bren guns, some hand grenades, and a bazooka. We had to be very careful with our supply of kerosene and solvents because of wartime shortages, and we had to be especially careful of fire.

One day while we were working, I asked these men about the attitude of the people living around us in the area.

"Or do they know about us?" Ted added.

"Some do," Bob answered, "but some of them cannot be trusted. There are a few Quislings — they are people who are sympathetic to the Germans — and the 'Blackies'."

"We learned about them lately, the older ones who are supposed to keep the peace, or something." I answered.

"Yea, and then, there are people who just can't help talking too much!" Joe interposed.

"So that is why we must be very careful. We do not want to put this family at risk, nor ourselves either." Frank laid a finished project in the pile. "So, we do this cleaning up here out of sight, because Germans walk right into the house without warning to barter for eggs and different food stuffs they want. Since we have to spend most of our daylight hours up here anyway, we might as well be busy helping out the Allied war effort."

I noticed that the Prinzen children were very disciplined, even the littlest who must have been about four years old. He was always watching the road and when he would see someone coming, anyone, he alerted the household some way, especially if they were Germans, and we would head for our hiding place if we were not already there.

During those days, we were not always under tension, and sometimes we would stick our heads out a door or window. This would, understandably, make Moeder very nervous since she had ten children to protect, so we tried to be discreet during the daytime and generally confined our exercise time to the night time hours.

There were fun incidents. Like the time I was in the toilet, which was out in the barn, and I suspect was erected for us evadees since we had to remain hidden inside the building. I was meditating when all of a sudden there was a big bang on the side of the little room. It seems that the whole Prinzen family was throwing potatoes at me, or trying to lob a potato through a small hole in the wall beside me. It scared me for a while, until I heard giggling and I knew I was the brunt of some Dutch fun.

There was another time when we were in the living room for a while. Marinus was at the table. On the table there were tobacco leaves, some kind of glue, and a wooden cigar mold for making five cigars at a time. He was busy rolling cigars as this was his assigned job. We were all sitting around watching him. I looked up from what I was examining. Marinus apparently left the room although I did not hear him leave. Then I saw a spiral of smoke coming up from under the table. I leaned over and saw little Marinus under the table sneaking smokes from a piece of cigar.

One humorous incident that I will always remember happened when I came out of the kitchen one Sunday morning and walked through the dell around the corner of the pump house, and Moeder and Truida were there, stripped to the waist washing themselves. I was very embarrassed and flustered, stumbled over my own feet, apologized and did an about-face to retrace my steps. I could hear the two women laughing and calling to me, "Vut's matter O-ven?" and I answered, "Oh nothing, nothing, nothing," and fled.

All of us enjoyed holding the little children on our laps now and then, and they seemed to enjoy our company too. All of us airmen took turns peeling potatoes, gathering eggs, and Bobby even decided one day that he needed to learn to milk a cow. Now Bobby was a city boy from San Francisco and he had never learned to milk a cow, but he was determined. He saw the terrible sores on the Prinzen boys' hands, partly due to the cold weather. It hurt them to milk the cows and the cows didn't like it either.

Truida and Hermein helped with the cooking and cleaning a lot and we helped, too, when we could. There were so many to feed. At this time there were seventeen, and extras if one or more members of the Dutch Underground were visitors at the house.

About a quarter of a mile down the road, the main group of the Dutch Underground for the area was staying. About thirty-five members of the Underground were living in an old barn, known as 'de Bark' with the Second-in-Command, Hendrick Van t'Lam. He was second in command to Jan Ket, who was the leader of the Underground. Because they lived and worked out of the barn, they were known as 'The Barkeans'.

'De Bark', 1945. Headquarters of the local Dutch Underground.

The Farm Somsenhuis

They practiced and exercised inside the barn with the guns to become familiar with the different weapons. We often went over there at night time to visit. Several of the Dutch could speak English and we were able to pick up a few words in Dutch while those who wished could practice their English skills with us.

There were a few close calls during these visits. One night, one of the Dutch fellows was handling a great big pistol, a Texas Ranger model with a chrome hexagon barrel. That barrel looked almost as long as a rifle barrel to me.

All of a sudden, "WHAM!" the gun went off. The bullet hit the brick wall behind us and splattered pieces of brick back on us, and for a second I thought I'd been hit.

"What the Hell are you doing?" I yelled. Then I realized it was brick splinters I got hit with instead of a bullet.

Another time, we were working on an old Harley-Davidson motorcycle, believe it or not! We were trying to get it to run for our Underground commander, Jan Ket, and it would backfire, but we couldn't get it started. Suddenly, "rat-tat-tat-tat!" and pieces of cement spattered around two fellows who had been sitting really close, towards the front where this Bren gun was resting. One of those young fellows had been practicing loading and unloading the clip and he accidentally pulled the trigger. It went off. This blew pieces of cement all around and we thought at first the battery of the motorcycle had blown up. Then we realized that this Bren gun had been fired. Someone could have been killed.

Guard duty was necessary around this barn at night, and just like any other military guard duty, we all took our turns. There were two soldiers in German uniforms who had contacted our commander. They told Jan that they were cooks in the German paratroopers. They felt that Germany was losing the war and since they were never sympathetic to the German cause, they wanted to defect. They were from Alsace-Lorraine and felt they were really French and not German. Anyway, they were forced into the German Army. I stood guard duty one night during our stay there. It seemed odd to be standing guard next to a person wearing a German uniform. We all took turns standing guard outside as well as inside. While on inside guard duty, we watched out the windows.

After returning to the Prinzen farm the night before, Frank, Ted and I were together in the attic room. Joe and Bob did not come back but stayed a few more days at the barn. I decided to ask Frank some things about himself.

"What part of England are you from, Frank?"

"I grew up in Brighton."

"Where is that?" asked Ted.

"On the southern coast of England," Frank said.

"Have you ever been to the United States?"

"Oh, yes. I was in your country for awhile teaching young RAF Cadets to fly. That was in the State of Georgia."

"How did you like the weather?" Ted asked.

"It was delightful. No cold weather, at least while I was there," Frank laughed.

"I don't think you have told us the story of how you got here. We have told you our story. How about it?" I asked.

"An excellent idea! It will fill in the time until the evening when we are free to move around more," Frank answered.

Chapter 5

Frank's Story

• • •

On September 27, 1944, we were flying a de Havilland DH-98 Mosquito quite high, close to the brilliant stars. There were two of us, Bombigator [bombardier/navigator] Ron Naiff*, and myself as pilot. We carried a 4,000 pound bomb on board, destination Berlin. First, we were ordered to take a long route by way of Karlsruhe to lure fighters away from the Lancasters' bombing of ball bearing facilities.

"It's a long trip to Berlin this way," Ron remarked from his position in the nose. He turned off the small light he had been using when checking his maps and instruments.

"Agreed," I answered, constantly scanning the sky, "But we have no choice. We must protect our Lancs [Lancaster bombers]."

A bright ribbon below glistened off and on as though secretly signaling.

"We've reached the Rhine, Frank. We will be over Karlsruhe very soon now." Our radar-equipped night fighters ahead of us began dropping colored flares to show the Mosquitos the way. A few minutes later, the horizon began to reveal quick explosions of light. The aura increased rapidly as we flew closer.

"Karlsruhe ahead," Ron muttered unnecessarily.

A few minutes later we could see the whole drama unfolding below us. Lancasters on their way to the target, others over the target dropping bombs, and still others, having dropped their loads, turned toward home. Messerschmitts and Focke-Wulfs trailed behind waiting to pick up the silhouettes of the Lancasters as they went over the search lights.

---

* In the original 1995 manuscript, the bombigator is referred to as Walter Bedford. However, Frank Dell, in his book, *Mosquito Down* (2014), indicates that his bombigator's name was Ron Naiff.

"Here we go," I nudged the right rudder, "Let's see if we can get them to fight."

Down we went to the grim parade below. The other Mosquitos spread out and made themselves equally vulnerable to the enemy's sights. The 109's and 190's turned to slap the Mosquitos down. The contests of skills raged as dozens of aircraft dipped, dived, and roared. The whole fierce scrap gradually moved north. Search lights switched on all along our way below.

There was a slight bump. I leaned forward to check my panel. The search lights were blinding me.

"Stay alert, Ron. I can't see my panel because of the lights."

"Roger," Ron answered, then, "We're coming near Münster," and a few seconds later, "Frank, our petrol is down. We must have picked up some flak. We'd better scratch."

"Heading home," I replied. I moved my back a little to relieve the tension and a searchlight hit me right in the face. The Mosquito jolted violently.

"Should I fasten on my 'chute?" Ron asked.

"I think I've got it under control," I answered, then I realized the engines were laboring, approaching a stall.

The next second the Mosquito reared up on its tail and fell off into a spin of about four or five gyrations. We cannot survive. Ron's chest 'chute is not attached. Wild thoughts of pain and regret flooded my mind. The plywood aircraft broke up. I found I was free of the pilot's seat, tumbling end over end. I did not know how I became free of the seat, as I was strapped into it just seconds before. I was falling, so I pulled the cord. 'Goodbye, my friend,' I thought, as I watched the pieces of the Mosquito crash and explode below. 'You should have quit when you completed your tour and not volunteered to fly with me.' I felt sick. I lost a good friend. I'll never forget him.

I landed just outside the city of Münster. It was about the same time as the British paratroop landings at Arnhem, I found out later. The whole sky was lit up by the gunfire around Arnhem, which I could see even though it was about a hundred miles away. The battle for Arnhem was raging. I collapsed my 'chute and discarded it under a clump of grass and set off on foot in the direction of that brightness in the sky, skirting the city. I crawled over and under fences, crossed canals and fields in the dark, stumbled and sometimes fell over uneven ground and an occasional railroad track.

For four rainy nights I walked. During the day, I found a place to hide. The first day, I hid in a haystack. The second day in a grove of trees. On the third day, it was an abandoned chicken house. On the fourth morning I found a barn behind a farmhouse in which to hide. I knew I was in Holland or close to it. I estimated I'd walked about twenty miles each night so must have covered more than eighty miles so far.

When I slipped into the barn, wet and chilled, the dry warm hay was irresistible. I found a secluded spot in the hay and removed my wet clothes and threw them into the corner hoping they might dry off a bit.

I was awakened at dawn by machine gun fire. I moved to the round window and looked out. A spitfire was shooting at a tank on the main road near the farm. There was a loud 'womp' as the tank exploded. I was just settling back in the hay when I heard stealthy footsteps coming up the ladder to the hayloft where I was hidden. The door at the top of the ladder squeaked softly as it was opened very slowly. I decided that whoever was there was as frightened as I was. I heard some excited whispering and I raised my head a little and peered through the hay. Two boys about sixteen years old had found my clothes and were holding pieces of my uniform in their hands. Not wanting to be captured in the nude, I shot out from my hiding place to claim my clothes.

The boys' eyes grew very large from the sudden encounter, but one lad recovered quickly and spoke in halting English, "You are English pilot?"

"Yes," I answered.

"The Germans from that truck are in our farm. You must be very quiet."

"I am in Holland then?"

"Yes, it is only two kilometers to the border. We cannot stay here any longer. Stay hidden. One of us will be back tonight. You have food?"

"No more I'm afraid. My rations are gone. I've been down four days and nights."

One boy spoke to his brother who climbed down and almost immediately returned carrying some raw potatoes and carrots apparently stored in the barn for the animals.

"We will bring more food later. Put these clothes near you and keep to the far side by the window," he said.

"Right! And thank you," I answered. I took my clothes and crawled back to my hiding place near the little round window. I burrowed deep under the hay covering myself completely. Later, I roused and ate a carrot then drifted off to sleep again.

That afternoon, I amused myself watching the comings and goings in the farm yard below. Apparently, there were Nazi officers attached to a tank unit lodging in the farmhouse. The two boys moved freely around the farm.

It was Monday and in the late afternoon a man on a bicycle rode down the driveway to the farm. 'Must be their father,' I decided. The two boys met him in the yard. I couldn't hear their voices, yet I knew the boys were telling their father about finding an English pilot in their barn. All three were careful not to look in my direction except one time the father put his hand on one boy's head probably to keep him from looking up at the little round window.

I felt very nervous. My clothes were dry, so I put them on and again burrowed under the hay, carefully covering myself. That night after dark, the hay loft door at the top of the ladder slowly opened.

"English pilot, are you there?" It was a man's whisper.

"I am here," I whispered back. I could hear the man crawling over the hay to my position near the window.

"I am Tor Janson. I am the school teacher in this area." He spoke perfect English. "Who are you?"

"I am Lieutenant Francis H. Dell," I answered.

"You have identification?"

"Yes, of course!" I immediately turned out my pockets. When Tor was satisfied, he handed everything back to me.

"Where are you headed?" he asked.

"I saw the bright sky in the direction of Arnhem. I supposed I might contact some of the British troops there and perhaps get back to England."

"The battle is going badly for the Allies at Arnhem. It is best you do not try. At any rate, it is quite dangerous." Tor's expression was very serious. "I know everyone in the village," Tor continued, "I am the teacher at the school. I will contact the right person tonight. If the way is clear, they will escort you to a safer place. We have Germans living in our home. You cannot stay here. Your contact will come after midnight. Stay here. He will identify himself by whistling." Tor tugged on his right ear lobe, then pursed his lips and softly whistled the first seven notes of 'Mary Had a Little Lamb'.

"When you hear the door to the hayloft open and someone whistles those notes, only then come out from under the hay and follow him quietly, doing exactly as he does."

"Right!" Tor shook my hand, saying nothing more. He closed the door and I could hear his steps down the ladder. A few seconds later, I heard the outside door of the barn close. I looked out the little round window and saw Tor enter the kitchen door to his house.

I burrowed back down in the hay. By my watch I had more than four hours 'til midnight. I thought it would seem like an eternity, but I fell asleep again.

When I woke up someone was opening the hayloft door very slowly. My stomach muscles tensed with excitement. I waited. The man was a very unskilled whistler, but the tune he whistled was unmistakable. I moved quickly across the hay and answered quietly, "I am here."

"Follow me," I was told. I could see no one, but I followed the footsteps down the ladder and saw the barn door was open when I could see the stars. I slipped through it as quietly as I could and closed the door softly behind me. A black figure grasped my right arm and whispered, "'Stay close!" Then my guide took me by the hand and led me across a pasture and through a grove of trees. We crossed a canal on a foot bridge and continued on over another grassy pasture to a ditch.

"Jump!" my guide ordered and together we cleared the ditch. Still holding my hand, my guide led me along a pathway, winding in and out of trees. 'Must be a park,' I thought.

My guide led me across a graveled area and up to a small shed.

"Here!" was whispered in my ear. The guide knocked on the door, paused, then opened the windowless shed. After closing the door behind him, someone lit a small lamp.

We were in a tool shed.

Joe

Two men sat on a bench along the wall. One in an American Army Air Force uniform and the other in dark clothing from his hat to his shoes.

"We can talk now — quietly, of course!" My guide turned to me.

"Your first name is Frank?"

I nodded.

"I am Kees. The American flyer is Joe. His companion is Willum."

We shook hands all around. Joe and I exchanged enthusiastic greetings and the two Dutchmen stepped a little away and began talking softly in Dutch.

"What goes, do ya' suppose?" Joe asked.

"I've no idea, unless they are planning their next move. I think we will ultimately be hidden on a farm near here," I answered. "What happened to you?"

"I just bailed out today. Boy! I thought sure the Krauts [Germans] were going to nab me, but these Dutchman, they are really something! I was hidden in this bushy area, see, and the Nasties [Nazis] were going all around me practically on foot and on motorcycles and didn't spot me. There wasn't a Dutchman to be seen, but they were there all right just the same. I found out later, one was up a tree with field glasses, another was watching from an upstairs window of the farmhouse nearby. When the Germans gave up to look elsewhere, Willum came into the bushes and dashed me off in the opposite direction and brought me here. Willum can't speak English and I can't speak any Dutch. I didn't know what was going on. They were obviously waiting for you."

Joe gesticulated a lot while he talked.

Kees and Willum joined us. "We will move on now," Kees said.

Frank's Story

"Willum will go ahead for safety. You must not talk, just follow me."

The lamp was extinguished. Willum went out the door. Kees waited a few seconds, then, "Come!" and led the way out of the shed. Joe and I stayed close behind Kees so we would not lose him in the dark. The sky was cloudy and looked threatening. The way twisted and turned, went across foot bridges and, at one point, came to a road. Kees put his forefinger across his lips.

"Shush!" he whispered and squatted down in the grass along the road. A German jeep-type vehicle came down the road. As it went by us, we could hear German soldiers singing a rousing tune.

When it appeared to be safe, Kees motioned for us to follow him. We soon saw the outline of a farmhouse in the early morning light. That is how we arrived at the Prinzen farm known as Somsenhuis.

· · · · ·

"That is quite a story, but what happened after you got here until Ted and I arrived?" I asked.

"Well, after we had rested for about two days, we joined the activities of the Dutch Underground under Jan Ket's command and, in no time at all, we were going out on the night drops.

"When we, Joe and I, were at the Prinzen farm for only a few days, the Underground sent a member to the farm to warn us that they believed the Prinzen family was under suspicion, so we were moved to another farm where we stayed for about two weeks.

"A black-uniformed Quisling-type (collaborator) sergeant came to that farm for something and the farmer got angry with the collaborator. The farmer was arrested and sent to a German labor camp. So the Underground came and took us back to the Prinzen farm.

"But to continue my story of the drops...."

· · ·

There is a code system used that comes over the BBC. The code indicates the date, time and place of a drop. The codes are quick phrases such as; 'A stitch in time saves nine'. 'Mary had a little lamb', or 'Santa Claus will come tonight'. All these code messages have particular significance for particular people. A code phrase might be, 'Mary had a little lamb.' That means, we are coming to your place tonight. Another phrase indicates the period of the night.

They never give the exact time, but simply say between midnight and 3 a.m., or between 3 a.m. and 5 a.m. or something like that. So, each day we listen to these code phrases after the BBC news, and if we hear our phrase, it is an alert. Then the procedure is to listen to the next news broadcast at six o'clock in the evening, and if our phrase is then again repeated, that means they are coming for sure. But we don't go on any more drops now since the front has moved so close.

Anyway, on most occasions, we got our message at midday and we got it again at 6 p.m. and we knew we were going, so we prepared. We all got guns of one sort or another to take with us. We got the farm cart and the farm horse, padded his hooves with sacking that wrapped around his hooves and tied to his ankles with string so that the padding could not come off. It took over an hour to get to the drop site. We never took the main roads. We always crossed on the lesser pathways. We led the horse so we could go as quietly as possible. The cart had rubber tires, so it didn't make any great noise.

One night when Joe was on one of these trips, he got the biggest gun he could find and a couple of magazines and goodness knows what, and before we got half-way to the drop-zone, he was absolutely tuckered out. Well, we took the gun and put him and his gun and all the other items he was carrying in the cart and went on our way. So that was a learning experience for him.

We each had a flashlight that was mounted in a box so that when the light was turned on, the light could not be seen from the ground, but only from the air.

After we arrived at the drop zone, we often had to wait about an hour or more before we would hear a familiar engine approaching. We would begin to wonder if the plane was coming at all, and in the still of the night we imagined hearing sounds that were not really there. I kept imagining that I could hear the plane coming. We would dash out very excited and nothing happened, so we went back to waiting again.

All the boys had these boxed-in flashlights except me. I had one of a larger size because, being the only one who knew the Morse Code, it was my job to flash the code letters in Morse Code to signal the airplane when it came. Those in the airplane would answer with the same code signal and then we each knew who the other was.

Well, eventually, the plane would come in, signals were exchanged and all of us used our flashlights so that there was a landing strip of sorts. The plane lined up for the drop run only about five hundred feet off the ground.

They did not pack those boxes very well sometimes and when they hit the ground, they would break open. We always felt we should put our hands over our heads for protection as boxes of chocolate, corned beef and dynamite came pouring out of the containers. These drops were carried by British Sterling bombers and I think they used twenty-six or twenty-seven big containers for each run.

Once they were all on the ground, we rolled up the parachutes, piled them and the containers on the farm cart, and prepared to push off back home. They were very heavy, those containers. It took four of us to lift one comfortably. I guess they must have weighed about three hundred pounds each.

This big field we used as a dropping zone was just a huge big farm field with little or nothing growing in it. The Germans used it as a rifle range. They had some targets set up at one far end. At the other end they would lie down and shoot at the target. At night, we used it as a dropping zone so that one way or another, the field was well utilized.

After each drop, we picked up everything we could find at first. We then had to be very sure there was nothing left in the field to be found the next day when the Germans held their manoeuvers.

· · · · ·

"How did you do that?" Ted asked. "It must have been awfully dark."

"Right! It was dreadfully dark," Frank agreed. "So, our method was this: We would get down on our hands and knees, interlock our arms and crawl the whole distance of the field, turn at the end and come back again covering another strip, until the entire area was covered. It was a bloody good decision because we occasionally found an item we missed the first time, such as a rifle or rifles sticking out of the ground barrel down in the mud. It was absolutely imperative that all items be located or the whole program could have collapsed since the Germans would have been alerted."

"What other incidents can you tell us about after you came here to Somsenhuis?" I asked.

• • •

One day we saw this fellow bail out within two or three miles of where we were standing. We could hear German Army trucks and motor bikes start up and they took off to find and capture him. This fellow kept drifting down in his parachute and was actually drifting towards our farmhouse. He disappeared behind some trees while he was still about a half mile away and we could see him no longer.

Black Jan and the two men with him went to see if they could locate him before the Germans did, but came back without success. I walked up the lane to meet them and the four of us walked back to the farm together, going up a lane where a haystack was located along side.

Just as we were coming level with this haystack, a couple of hundred yards from the farmhouse, two German soldiers on bicycles popped around the corner nearby coming straight towards us. As they came around the corner and sort of straightened out, one of these Dutchmen butted me sideways behind this haystack. The Germans came up to these chaps and pulled out their machine pistols and said, "Hands up! Now have you seen an American pilot around here?"

"American pilot? No!" they answered, feigning surprise. I was having kittens!

Anyway, that was that. They seemed satisfied and got back on their bicycles and went off down the lane. We went back to the farm and the search was on all afternoon and evening. By nightfall, it was quite evident that they had not found this guy. Black Jan got eight or ten of the local

Frank's Story

farm people to gather in the farm kitchen. He explained to me that he was going into the woods again during the hours of darkness and they were going to have a good search for the pilot. None of them spoke English. Black Jan intimated to me that I should teach them some English phrases so that they could call them out as they walked about looking for this guy.

So all of these farmers sat around in a circle in that kitchen while I had them repeat over and over again, 'Come out, you silly bugger, we are your friends!'

After a while, these boys went out and searched up and down the woods calling these phrases all night long. The following morning, they came back with no success at all.

However, this pilot was brought to our farmhouse about three days later, having made contact with somebody else who was introduced to a doctor who knew a friend and so on. When he came to this farm, he said, "You know, the first night I was in the woods, the strangest things were going on! All these fellows were marching up and down shouting, 'Come out you silly bugger, we are your friends', but I knew those German tricks!"

Joe and I went into town a couple of times with Jan Ket. We went to visit with his friends and to show them that he was helping the Allies. He hoped that they would help out with food and other essentials after realizing the effort he was giving to the cause.

One day when we were relaxing in the hay, Jan told us that he was speaking to a forest ranger that morning. He said he would soon turn another pilot over to me who flew an aircraft like Joe's. His name is Bobby.

There are some more activities to relate that occurred after Bob's arrival, so why don't we hear his story when he returns from 'de Bark'. He was very active in the ammunition drops and many other projects.

• • • • •

"We can go down and get some exercise since its dark now. Let's go!" Ted called as he started down the ladder. We followed close behind.

'De Bark' worked out very well as headquarters for the Underground. It was located in an area where it was surrounded on three sides by a thick grove of trees and set well back from the road. It was a remote location.

Between the barn and main house, there was a large pasture. The main road could be seen in the distance, with clear visibility in both directions. A long straight driveway on level ground was easy to monitor.

The next day Jan Ket brought a pair of hand-made shoes for me that were my size since he had measured my feet soon after I arrived at Somsenhuis. They were made of leather, but since the shoemaker had no nails, he put the soles on with wooden tacks. It was a great relief for my feet. The shoes were very comfortable. He stayed in the loft with us that night.

Next morning, we were all sitting around the kitchen. Jan perched on the old organ stool clad in black leather, knee-length boots, black jodhpurs and a sleeveless undershirt. His suspenders, still fastened to his britches, dangled nearly to the floor behind him. A worn, dark blue flannel shirt and a black leather jacket rested neatly over the back of a nearby chair. An American Colt .45 rested in its holster on the chair seat.

With soap suds covering the lower half of his face, he sharpened the straight razor on a heavy strop securely fastened to the wall as the towel over his shoulder moved back and forth in rhythm. He ceased his stropping to test the razor's sharpness on a small patch of hair on his arm. Satisfied, he turned toward the window to utilize what winter daylight there was coming through the lace curtains. He had propped a piece of mirror precariously between two hymn books on the organ's top.

When he made his first downward stroke with the razor, he sensed, without really seeing, a movement outside the window. He began to whistle softly the simple tune that was the prearranged signal of danger. We all dropped to the floor. Jan slowly wiped a blob of soap suds onto the towel then dropped it over the gun in the chair. He saw a German soldier heading for the front of the house. Knowing they all walked right in without warning, he opened the window and leaned out on the window sill making himself as large as possible and called to him.

Meanwhile, we slipped out and went back to our hideout in the hayloft, but not before we heard Jan shout to the soldier, "Ja!" then he added, "I'll open the door for you."

Up in the loft, Frank quietly told us the soldier was apparently after some food, but sometimes that was a ploy by the Germans to check up on the Dutch citizens to see if they were up to anything that could be classified as against the Third Reich.

The following night when Ted, Frank and I were in the living room with the family, Bob and Joe returned from 'de Bark'. It was a pretty busy household. Truida and her mother had just finished the dishes and cleaned up the kitchen and were seated by the *kachel* (heating stove) darning the heavy socks used to wear with the *klompens* (wooden shoes). We tried wearing those wooden shoes and we found them to be very comfortable and warm. Moeder had an old-fashioned heating box that had hot irons heated from the stove. She put her feet on this box to keep her feet warm while she was repairing the socks. The old saying 'Men work from sun to sun and women's work is never done,' certainly rang true here. Moeder and Truida worked from early morning to late at night and though the men worked very hard during the day and were up very early, when it was evening, they tended to relax. Of course, Papa washed the dishes many times in the evening and all of us helped too, quite a lot.

Anyway, I asked Joe if he would tell us his story of how he got to Somsenhuis.

"I have told them what happened when you and I met," said Frank to Joe, "But I do not know myself what happened from the time you were in trouble with your P-51 until we came across each other."

"My experience is very similar to Bob's," Joe answered, "So why don't we hear Bob's story instead?"

"OK." Bob sat down, and the children sat close by eager to hear, knowing they would not understand it all, but they wanted to hear it anyway.

Chapter 6

Bobby's Story

• • •

On October 28, 1944, I flew my P-51 as part of a fighter escort for a bombing mission over Münster, Germany. I felt pride and excitement and it felt good. I had my own airplane. This change raised me to Element Leader instead of a wing man. My airplane sported the name 'San Francisco Mama' in honor of my home town. Now I could do the fighting with a wing man to protect my tail for a change!

In the distance I could see the city. Flak puffs from anti-aircraft guns were bursting all around the bombers. No one had yet been hit. As the bomber stream drew nearer the target, I saw occasional flak bursts closer around me. Suddenly, the fighter jerked and jolted. 'Mama' was hit! I glanced at the oil pressure gauge. It indicated there was no pressure. Then I noticed that the temperature gauge was climbing.

I felt panic rising in my throat, but my intensive training took control. I adjusted the power setting so that the engine would run as long as possible. I glanced through the wind screen noting there was a small amount of grayish-white smoke coming from the rear of the engine. I switched on the VHF.

"Blue Leader from Element Two! Blue Leader from Element Two! Come in Blue Leader!"

"Blue Leader here. You have a little smoke coming from your engine. Better head for home." The voice was calm — deliberately calm.

"Roger! I've got no oil pressure, and it's getting hot!" I banked to the right and headed toward the English Channel. Then black, blinding smoke clouded my wind screen and I knew if I stayed with 'Mama' any longer she might turn into a burning coffin.

"Blue Leader from Element Two! I'm bailing out!"

"Understood! Wing man for Element Two," Blue Leader's voice was still calm. The wing man acknowledged. "Stay with him until you see his 'chute open."

I unhooked myself from the VHF, nosed 'Mama' down to get below 10,000 feet, then trimmed the craft with a nose high attitude and released the canopy. I flung off my oxygen mask. The wind carried it away, then I rolled 'Mama' to bail out. Half-way out of the cockpit my harness straps hung up on the canopy track. I hung helplessly upside down. The slipstream's unrelenting force slammed the upper half of my body repeatedly against metal.

'God help me!' I prayed. The fighter went into a spin pinning me against the fuselage like water in a whirling bucket. Then I blacked out.

Miraculously, I came to, falling free. Instinctively, I reached for the rip cord, but a shock of pain moved up my right arm. I could not lift it to the ring. I managed to grasp my right wrist with my left hand then painfully lift my right arm until I could grip the ring. I pulled hard. The tearing agony in my right arm felt like I had torn it apart. The 'chute opened and jerked my neck. Nausea flooded my stomach and then quickly passed as I floated down through the clear, cold air. The wind passing through the parachute shrouds made an eerie, shrill whistle. I looked below and estimated I was about twenty-four hundred feet above the ground.

The sound of motors caught my attention. Two soldiers on motorcycles were racing to where I would probably land. A small patch of bright, green grass surrounded by darker green trees came up fast. I landed in a half roll recovering in a sitting position and easily collapsed my parachute.

I unhooked my harness and removed my helmet. I took inventory of myself — pain in left leg, right arm, back of neck and I felt slightly dizzy. I could see in the distance people running across the pasture in my direction.

'Friend or enemy?' I wondered, and reached for my Colt .45. I stood up, took a step toward the running figures and unexpectedly crashed to the ground on my face. A sharp, explosive pain shot up the bridge of my nose. I blacked out the second time.

I awakened in a fog of pain. My left knee hurt worse than before and I could taste blood oozing from my numbed nose. I soon realized I was being carried. Strong, gentle hands carefully lowered me to the ground on a mattress of hay. I felt the chill of a damp cloth. Someone was washing my face with tender care. I opened my eyes and looked into a pair of anxious blue ones which registered relief that I was conscious. A man in a bulky coat and heavy knitted cap knelt on one knee beside me. He held a bloody cloth in his left hand. He gestured with his right arm in a semi-circle.

"H-o-l-l-a-n-d," he said, pronouncing it slowly. He repeated the word and then the gesture after first pointing to me. I glanced at the man's foot near me and noted the wooden shoe. I tried to smile then closed my eyes and relaxed in the hay.

A guttural shout startled me and I looked straight into two rifle barrels. Two soldiers motioned me to get to my feet and put up my hands. The Dutch people had backed away.

Painfully, I got to my feet balancing most of my weight on my right foot. I raised my left hand, but only spread the fingers of my right hand. The two soldiers roughly searched me, but they found only my escape kit. They pocketed the cigarettes, chocolates, and K-rations and threw the container to the ground. One pulled my wristwatch off my arm and slipped it on his own wrist.

Dizziness enveloped me again and I collapsed in the hay. When I opened my eyes I watched, puzzled. The two soldiers were searching each of the Dutch people. Then I remembered I'd had a gun a few minutes before. They didn't find it. Finally, one of the soldiers angrily barked an order and two of the Dutch picked me up and carried me to one of the motorcycles. I could see its slit eye blinking at me as the morning sun glistened on the head lens. The motors were restarted and we moved off across the pasture. In the other motorcycle a soldier kept a rifle aimed at my head. I glanced over my left shoulder. 'Put the gun to good use,' I silently begged. I turned to my right and waved goodbye to the Dutch people in a sort of salute.

The motorcycles bumped up and down over the uneven ground. With each bump and jerk, pain shot through my left knee. A joint in my knee jolted out of place. I leaned forward and grasped my knee with my left hand to steady it and it popped back into place, easing the pain somewhat.

The driver maneuvered the throttle and the bumping smoothed out. I looked around. We were on a narrow, tree-lined, brick road. In the distance I could see a cluster of houses. Along the road people stopped and watched as the motorcycles sped along. Many furtively held up two fingers forming the 'V' sign for victory.

When we entered the little village, the cyclists turned to the left and stopped in front of a small building that looked different from the colorful little cottages. I decided that it must have been a school house. My driver stopped the motor, got off, and walked around to my side of the vehicle. He unfastened the side car door and reached out to help me. I waved him away. I grasped the edge of the car with my good left hand, stepped out on the brick road with my right foot, and stood up. I tried my left foot, stumbled, and the soldier caught my arm and assisted me up the two steps and through the door. Once inside I again shook off the help and managed by myself.

I'd already noticed the emblem on the sleeves of the soldiers' coats as replicas of ack-ack guns. Upon entering the front door of the building, I saw a command chart on the hall wall bearing the same emblem. 'Anti-Aircraft Battalion Headquarters', I figured as I was halted before a fat sergeant sitting behind a desk. The sergeant's body overflowed the chair. His hair was very blond and his face was florid and puffy. He'd been watching my very painful approach.

"You need *doktor*?" he shouted.

"No." 'Do any of them ever speak in a soft voice?' I thought. The sergeant grunted and gestured to the guards who nudged me to an open door at the end of a hall. I paused in the doorway. It was about six by eight feet and was empty except for a blanket on the floor.

There was what my grandmother used to call a 'pottie' in one corner. A drop-light fixture holding a small single bulb hung from the ceiling. In the upper third part of the door was a small window about four by eight inches, containing no glass. One of the guards nudged me with his rifle and I moved forward. The door was closed behind me and the room was plunged in almost complete darkness. There was a click of a key. I was locked in. I groped for the light string and was grateful when the dim light came on. Then I lay down on the blanket, rolled up in it and was soon asleep.

The Bluff

A short while later, I woke up to the sound of the sergeant's bellowing voice. My whole body was stiff and sore. I turned over on my back and used my left arm for a pillow. I thought over what had happened. I didn't relish being a prisoner, and why had I refused medical aid? I recalled a story I had heard back in England about a pilot who bailed out in France and was taken prisoner. The Underground came to him and managed to slip him a note and some chewing tobacco. The note instructed him to chew the tobacco and swallow it. It would cause the same symptoms as appendicitis. He did. Sure enough, he was taken to a hospital for an appendectomy. It slowed his getting out, but the Underground managed it.

If I could get into a hospital, maybe someone would help me, I reasoned. I sat up and started yelling for a doctor. In a few minutes the door opened and the sergeant stuck his head in.

"*Was ist los?*" he roared.

I screwed up my face in pain grasping my left knee and moaned, "Doctor!"

"*Nein!*" The door was shut again and locked.

Strike one, I thought, and sat there trying to remember the briefings on survival back at the base. 'The Germans are accustomed to strict military procedure,' the briefing officer had said, 'and in dealing with them, pull rank and they will respect you for it'.

I began yelling again until the sergeant's face appeared at the little window.

"*Ja?*" he scowled.

"I am an officer and a gentleman, and I demand to see an officer of equal rank, and a doctor." I spoke clearly and with as much dignity as I could. The sergeant said something unintelligible. His face disappeared from the window, yet several minutes later, the door opened and two soldiers came in with a litter. They tied my hands and feet, lifted me onto the litter and carried me out to an ambulance just driving up to the front of the building.

Bobby's Story

They carried me across the small lobby of the hospital to a desk and propped the litter up between two chairs. I sat up. A middle-aged, motherly-looking woman sat in a chair behind the desk smiling at me. She was dressed in a neat, Red Cross uniform.

"Hello," she said in a soft, friendly tone. "I'm here to help you." Her American accent and soft voice were soothing to my ears. "You'll be seeing the doctor soon, but in the meantime, I would like to let your family know you are OK. What is your name, Lieutenant, and your serial number?"

"Robert W. Brown, Ma'am, AO 735026."

"Thank you, Bob. May I call you Bob?" she asked, and wrote the information on the form in front of her. It was not really a question, since she seemed unconcerned about my answer. She laid her pen down and opened a drawer where she withdrew a package of cigarettes and a box of wooden matches.

"Smoke?" she asked. I nodded. She removed a cigarette from the pack. "Seen any of your friends from San Francisco lately? I'm from there myself." She reached across her desk and put one end of the cigarette in my mouth.

"A beautiful city, isn't it, Bob?" I didn't answer. "Of course, I'll need more information so that I can notify your family." She removed a wooden match from the box, struck the side of the matchbox and the match burst into flame. Slowly her hand moved toward me, then paused.

"Where were you headed when you had to bail out?" she asked. Her tone was light, friendly, but her blue-gray eyes glittered in the flame. I couldn't recall any briefings to cover this situation. Alarm bells kept ringing in my head. She touched the flame to the tip of the cigarette. I immediately inhaled.

"I am Lieutenant Robert W. Brown, Serial Number AO 735026," I repeated.

"What was your mission, Lieutenant?" She blew out the match. I inhaled again.

"That's all I'm allowed to tell you, Ma'am," I stared steadily at her through the smoke. Gradually her expression changed to frustration, then anger. She snatched the burning cigarette from my mouth, put it out in a nearby ash tray and opened the desk drawer. With a sweeping motion of her arm, the cigarettes and matches disappeared into its depths. She slammed it shut, signaled the guards and abruptly turned her back on me.

The guards came forward, picked up the litter and carried me from the room. Before going through the double doors at the back of the lobby, I turned my head and looked back. She was watching me leave, a frown on her face. I sent her a painful grin.

The soldiers carried me across the hall into a room about eight by ten feet. There were glass windows on the hall side, but no outside windows. A skylight in the ceiling told me it was well past midday. The guards stopped next to a cot, the only one in the room, and helped me onto it. They untied me, picked up the litter and left, locking the door behind them.

I lay back, pleased to discover there was even a little pillow. The only other piece of furniture in the room was a bare, unpainted footstool beside the bed. It wasn't much, but it was more than I'd had before. I slowly checked around the room and I noticed a door at the far corner.

I glanced up and down the hall. I saw no one around. I eased my good foot to the floor and hobbled to the wall. The dizziness was back and there was a steady hammering in my head. I leaned against the wall until my head cleared, then moved toward the door. I grasped the doorknob and slowly opened the door. It was a completely furnished bathroom with another, smaller skylight.

I blew a soft whistle of admiration. 'I'll bet I don't stay here very long,' I said to myself, then caught my reflection in the mirror. The black and blue protrusion in the middle of my face used to be a fairly well-shaped nose, and there was dried blood on the side of my head. Beneath my wild, black hair, my face was pale under its tan. My eyes were bloodshot and outlined with angry bruises.

I stuck out my tongue at the apparition, winced in pain, and turned back to the dubious comfort of the cot. I hoped to see the doctor soon. My head ached, my knee hurt, and my right arm felt like it was not quite in its socket. I felt shaky and empty. I suddenly realized I hadn't eaten since before dawn back at the base in England. Mostly I was tired!

Bobby's Story

Hospital

I was lying on my left side with my eyes closed. I was half asleep. It seemed I was in a more comfortable bed and there were strange sounds in the room full of people. Some were breathing steadily while others were talking in low tones. I couldn't understand one word. There were smells, too, of cigarette smoke, blood, urine, germs and wood smoke.

Suddenly, there was a sound of metal clanging against metal. I was startled fully awake. Near my bed an elderly man, wearing heavy winter clothing, was bent over a pot-bellied stove lighting a match to the contents inside.

I stared in disbelief, then slowly looked around the room. This was no dream! I counted the number of beds. Twelve, including my own. I shifted my body and felt a tight bandage and sling harness fastened around my neck and waist that held my right shoulder and arm immobile. My left hand went to my injured knee. No bandage. It was badly swollen, though, and was sore to the touch. I eased myself on my back. The only windows in the room were in the wall near my bed.

Then I remembered! The doctor and an officer had come. The officer asked questions while the doctor worked, but I kept falling asleep. I hoped I was uncooperative. I also remembered having some black bread and coffee. By the empty feeling in my stomach, that was at least two days ago. I wished I could have a cup of coffee and a cigarette! I hoped those two who stole my cigarettes choked on them, but then, how about the guy who stole my watch! I noticed my uniform was folded and lying on a stool at the head of my bed. There should be a packet of cigarette papers and a small box of matches in the shirt pocket I'd put there before I left the base. I felt the shirt. The papers were still there, but I didn't have any tobacco anyway.

The breakfast trolley caught my attention, but it was at the far end of the room and I knew I would be last to get any food or water. I tried to relax and draped my arm over the edge of the bed. The clank and clatter at the stove stopped. Something was slipped gently into the curve of my fingers. I didn't move except to close my fingers a little.

A cigarette! I slowly drew my left hand back under the rough blanket and up to my chest. I glanced up at the old man, who smiled, secretly made a 'V' sign with his fingers and went away. I reached for the small box of matches when I remembered another story of the flyer who was slipped a message with some tobacco that ultimately led to his escape.

I swore as I stared at the cigarette, torn between ripping it apart to see if there was a message inside and lighting it to enjoy a smoke. Finally, under cover of the blanket I tore the cigarette into shreds. I went through the loose tobacco thoroughly. No message. I retrieved the tobacco, then the papers and matches from my uniform. With some difficulty I finally rolled myself a smoke. After lighting it, I lay back on the cot trying to forget my disappointment and the empty feeling in my guts. I enjoyed the smoke even through bruised nostrils.

'I've got to get out of here. The sooner the better,' I thought. If they didn't get the right answers, they'll question me again. Besides these guys could kill me in my sleep!'

I stole a look at the soldier in the next bed, who was asleep. I knew I couldn't get very far with my injured knee, but I was sure that when I improved enough, I'd be moved to a prison camp where escape was harder, or so I'd heard. I decided my shoulder must not be broken since it wasn't in a cast. I already noticed the two windows near my bed opened up like double doors, but were solidly locked from the outside by means of a board nailed across the window pane.

Plans for Escape

So I began to form a plan as I watched the smoke drift slowly toward the ceiling. I would perfect a plan of sleep in short naps, and when sleeping, I would keep my head covered so that any time anyone looked my way all they could see was a form on the bed. Under cover of the blanket, I would carefully slip my arm out of the harness and slowly exercise it, tense my muscles, and move my arm up and down a little more each time. Then I would carefully return the harness to its former position.

I put this plan in motion right away and whenever the food trolley was brought, I broke off a piece of hard, black bread from my tray and hid it in one of the pockets of my uniform. During the day I went to the latrine as many times as I could get the nurse to help me. My right arm and shoulder were painful, my left knee was still swollen and sore. I had a dull headache all the time and my nose hurt. Every time I went to the latrine, I tried to put a little more weight on my left foot. I wore only my shorts and tightened up all my muscles and moaned and groaned as I made my way from bed to bed to impress anyone who might be watching. No pretense was necessary. The pain was real.

'Fritz', as I mentally dubbed him, slept in the next bed. He didn't seem to be wounded in any way so I decided he was there as my guard. I never spoke to him. His favorite pastime was taking the Dutch girls home who worked in the hospital. As he left with one of them, he would toss a triumphant leer at me. I glared in return. I didn't have the relief of feeling safe when 'Fritz' left either. All the German soldiers in the room had side arms. I knew that any one of them would shoot me for the slightest excuse. Every night before going to bed, 'Fritz' unloaded his Luger, cleaned it, reloaded it, then he'd pull a scissor-action with it. It would pop off with a nerve-shattering click. 'Fritz', stone faced, watched me steadily all the while.

Each morning the old Dutchman who lit the fire slipped a cigarette to me, gave his secret sign for victory and went away. Each morning while I smoked my cigarette, I planned the day's strategy.

One morning, after six days, though my shoulder was still sore, I decided it was usable, and my knee was well enough. To wait longer might mean a careful examination from a medic who would undoubtedly pronounce me well enough to vacate my bed and I'd be on my way to prison camp and perhaps an uncomfortable interrogation.

When night came, I pretended to sleep. I had to be sure everyone else was asleep before I made my move. Before long, I was fighting to stay awake. Next thing I knew, it was morning.

While the smoke from my morning cigarette swirled over my head, I pondered the problem. I needed one more day. The only solution was to have a full bladder. I knew I couldn't sleep in that condition. As before, I made my five or six trips to the latrine, but didn't urinate. By the time night came, it was impossible for me to sleep. I lay under the blanket wide awake and miserable until all was quiet. The only light in the room was from four dim night lights, each located near the ceiling, one on each wall. I made my move.

I slipped the harness off my shoulder and shoved it down to the foot of the bed under the covers with my foot. I held my dog tags in my hand to keep them still while I slipped them off over my head. I couldn't have them jingling at the wrong time. I moved off the bed, then bunched my covers up around my pillow to look like a sleeping form. I put on my uniform and moved cautiously to the next bed where 'Fritz' was sleeping peacefully. I stole his sweater, scarf, and wool socks then slowly made my way toward the exit at the opposite corner of the room. Then I remembered my dog tags! They were lying in full view on top of my 'sleeping form'.

"Damn dummy!" and added a string of obscene oaths under my breath as I retraced my route, put the dog tags in my pocket, crouched between my bed and the wall, and struggled into the sweater, scarf and socks. Now my feet made no sound on the wooden floor but I'd lost my desire to stand upright. Trying to ignore the pain, I began crawling close beside each bed. I paused and listened intently to the breathing of each occupant.

When I reached the width of the room and was turning the corner to crawl the length to the door, one of the soldiers suddenly sat up in bed and pointed a pistol directly at me. I smothered a rising desire to scream in terror just as the apparition disappeared. Cold sweat trickled down the sides of my face as I continued toward the door.

I reached the last bed, removed a pair of hob-nailed boots from the floor and carefully rose to my feet and lifted a heavy jacket from a nail on the wall. With that over one arm and a heavy boot in each hand, I headed toward the door. I planned to use the boots as clubs if necessary, should the guard be outside the door. I knew the guard was usually there. I'd seen him several times when workers or visitors came through the door.

Calling on the Almighty for help, I opened the door. No one was there. A murmur of voices and an occasional feminine giggle behind the door to the right, however, told me the guard was making an early morning visit to the nurse's room. I limped rapidly across the hall to the next door. I opened it. I was outside! The biting cold was a relief. I closed the door quietly and breathed in the free air.

A harsh voice shouting something from inside the building panicked me and gave my injured leg wings. I bolted some forty yards across the road and flung myself headlong into a watery ditch. My nerves were taut and my fear so great that I had forgotten my bad leg. As my fear subsided, the pain returned. I lay there panting in the cold water and waited, listening. No sounds! Nothing! I crawled out on the opposite bank and onto the grass. A painful cramp in my bladder gave warning. I urinated and some of the tension left me. Now I was aware even more of a throbbing pain in my knee.

'Don't quit on me now!' I begged the complaining joint and massaged it with both hands. I could hear the guns of war in the distance and the sky in that direction displayed occasional bursts of light. I headed toward the light, limping along the wet grass parallel with the road. Each time I crossed a canal I stopped, emptied the big boots, then continued on.

Nearly every field contained a farmhouse. Once, I saw a farmer going the other way pushing a cart of milk cans. The farmer gave no indication that he was aware of my presence, but I crouched close to the ground anyway. Who could I trust?

Finally, it was light enough to see distant trees. I was tired and chilled. I was mostly dragging my leg along now. I had to find a place to rest and hide for the day. I munched on the last piece of dry bread. Another farmhouse came into view. It was a quiet, peaceful landscape dotted with haystacks here and there. I studied the house. A dim, friendly light shone through a window. 'I'd bet it's nice and warm in there,' I thought. A wave of homesickness swept over me. I shook it off and turned toward one of the haystacks. A dog barked. I froze.

"Shut up! Shut up!", I muttered softly but the dog continued to sound the alarm.

The farmhouse door opened. A man and woman, a boy and girl in their teens, and an old woman leaning on a cane came out into the yard. When they saw me they helped me into the house and pointed me to a chair in the kitchen. The young girl brought me a steaming cup of ersatz coffee flavored with sweet fresh cream.

"Thank you," I said. I could have kissed her I was so happy to be in a warm room. I held the cup with both hands to catch the heat. The family gathered at the opposite end of the kitchen and talked quietly among themselves occasionally looking in my direction.

"I'm a pilot," I said and set down the steaming cup. I spread my arms waving them up and down like a wounded albatross, "And I bailed out!" I put the palms of my hands together in front of me with my fingers pointing to the floor and wavered my hands downward.

"I was in a German hospital. I escaped! I need help!" They stared, saying nothing.

"*Spreken* English?" I asked. No answer.

"*Spreken* English?" I repeated louder. Still no answer.

"*SPREKEN* ENGLISH?" I shouted. They looked at each other. The farmer left the room. The boy and girl gathered their school books together and laid them down by the door then joined the two women at the opposite end of the table. They sat close together and watched me silently. I drank the hot liquid. The farmer soon returned with another man who was dressed in a neat, but well-worn, brown suit.

"*Dokter*," said the farmer then gestured to his family who followed him from the room. When the door closed, the doctor sat down beside me at the table.

Bobby's Rescue

"*Spreken* English?" I asked anxiously.

"*Ja*, you are Tommy [a British soldier], or Yank?"

"I'm a Yank. What a relief! It would be easier if I could speak Dutch, but I can't. I couldn't seem to make the family understand my problem."

"They all understand English except for the old one, but we are cautious to admit we can speak English. It can be dangerous. They thought at first you were a German airman. You are wearing German clothing," he pointed out. "And when you tried to say words that were not English, they knew you were not German." He smiled.

"I guess I got so damn tired, I'd forgotten about the clothing," I said and unfastened the jacket and removed it, then pulled the sweater off over my head. "You can see I'm wearing my uniform, but almost everything else was stolen from me."

"They realize you are an Ally, but they cannot help you. The old woman talks too much. If the Germans heard about you, they would kill the whole family. There is nothing they can do but take you back to the Germans. Because I am a doctor, it is expected that I speak several languages. That is why they sent for me."

'Remember, in Europe, the people consider the military a highly honorable profession and they have great respect for it,' the briefing officer had said.

I jumped to my feet and saluted, "My duty as an officer of the United States Army is to escape. I did once and I can do it again!"

After a startled pause, the older man jumped up and stood at attention, "Then it is my duty as a Dutch citizen to help you escape!" Again, he smiled and we both sat down. I wasn't sure if the doctor was serious or kidding me.

"Do you need my professional help?" asked the doctor.

"I've got a stiff, sore knee and shoulder, but I'm better than I was when I went into the hospital," I told him, and removed my shirt and rolled up my pant leg. The doctor examined me, then opened the bag he had left on the table when he came. He removed an elastic bandage and carefully wrapped my knee and fastened it with a metal clip. "Your knee should be higher than your head whenever possible. You may have trouble with it for a long time. Your shoulder will be well if you are careful."

The doctor left the room and a few minutes later returned with the farmer who was carrying a blanket, a bottle of water and a small bucket.

"We will hide you for today," the doctor said and handed me the sweater and jacket. "Except for him and his wife," the doctor nodded toward the farmer, "the family believe you have returned to the hospital."

They led me out into the yard. It was light now but everything was shrouded in a low ground mist. They stopped at one of the haystacks. The farmer brushed aside some hay at the bottom revealing a hole in the ground beneath. I learned later that every farmer had a secret place where they hid things from the Germans. I wrapped myself in the blanket and crawled in. There was only room to lie down curled up. The farmer set the bottle and the bucket beside me.

"You must keep very quiet. I will try to make contact with the

Underground," the doctor told me, then added, "Remember, this family understands English, but cannot speak it well enough to be understood." The farmer brushed the hay back in place. About an hour later the farmer returned and gave me a sandwich. For the rest of the day I shivered in the blanket.

As evening approached, the farmer appeared again and gave me a cup of warm milk fresh from the cow. I gratefully thanked him, and the farmer left again. Later, after sundown, the doctor appeared, riding one bicycle and pulling another one by the handlebars. I crawled out of the haystack.

"Can you ride?" the doctor asked, "We must ride five or six kilometers."

I stretched my cold stiff limbs. "Maybe it will warm me up. Let me limber up this knee a little first." The doctor watched while I limped up and down.

"You are ready?"

I nodded, and the doctor led the way down the driveway toward the main road. I had to hurry to keep pace. The oversized boots were awkward and the bicycle wavered drunkenly. I remembered the last time I rode a bike. I was on a Sunday jaunt in Golden Gate Park, a million years ago.

After about a mile, I got the hang of it again and soon got limbered up, almost warm, but a cold wind whistled around my uncovered ears. I tried to concentrate on keeping the doctor in view. I could see him dimly in the starlight. Suddenly, I skidded to a stop and looked back. The doctor was standing beside his bicycle along the edge of the road.

"We cross the canal here and enter the house of the forest ranger," the doctor said.

We pushed our wheels down through the canal water and up the other side. I emptied my big boots again and we continued on over the pasture grass toward a small grove of trees.

"We leave the bicycles here and walk now. We must be quiet." The doctor spoke softly. We moved cautiously through the trees. The doctor stopped and whispered a barely audible, "Wait here," in my ear and disappeared.

I hugged close to a tree and waited, trying to breathe noiselessly. In a few minutes there was a soft crunching noise. I held my breath, but it was the doctor returning with another man, big and broad-chested.

"Come," the doctor beckoned.

I followed them through the trees, across a small grassy, treeless area to the door of a large house. The ranger held the door open and we all entered. He closed the door and led us through another door. There were lights inside, but black blinds lined the windows.

"There are German officers in there," the ranger whispered, pointing to the door, "and a whole battalion of soldiers in the forest."

My back began to crawl with a thousand nerve endings. The ranger led us through the room and another door. He turned left and opened yet another door. A dim light hung from the ceiling. On the floor was a large wash tub half-full of hot water. On a wooden stand beside the tub was an enamel wash pan, a cloth, towel, toothbrush, a tube of Colgate toothpaste — the 50-cent size that I hadn't been able to buy in the States for two years — and a razor.

The doctor turned to me and shook my hand gently. "I leave you here," he said, "I have a patient nearby I must see. You are in good hands."

I grasped the doctor's shoulder. "Thank you, my friend, thank you!"

The doctor smiled, nodded to the ranger and left.

"I am Henry Van Lom," the big man whispered. "You bathe. I go to fix your hiding place. I will be back soon." He went away too.

I dipped enough hot water with the enamel pan from the tub to shave and brush my teeth and set it aside. I removed my clothes and sank down into that wonderful hot water. The warmth of the water soaked in and the aches and pains of my body responded soothingly. I relaxed. In no time I was jerking awake. 'No time for sleep now,' I thought. I quickly finished my bath and stepped out of the tub and rubbed myself briskly before dressing. I just finished brushing my teeth and shaving when the door opened quietly.

"Good, you are ready." Henry picked up the toothbrush and toothpaste and stuck them in his shirt pocket. "Come," he said and led the way back outside across the small grassy yard and into the trees. In a few steps we stopped.

"All you need is under there." Henry pointed to an opening beneath neatly stacked logs. "I will be back tomorrow night." He reached in his pocket and handed me the toothbrush and toothpaste. From another shirt pocket he pulled out a packet of cigarettes and matches. I accepted them with enthusiasm.

"Look before you smoke," he cautioned and disappeared.

Inside the hiding place, I found there was a thick layer of clean straw on the ground and about four feet of headroom. I felt around in the dark and discovered a treasure of useful items: two warm blankets, a package of sandwiches, a thermos of hot soup, a bottle of water to drink, and a sanitation bucket. I was in a space of about eighteen inches by thirty-six inches. I could just stand on my knees in there.

The weather behaved so I didn't have to sleep in water. I cleared a patch of straw away from one corner for smoking safety. The extra straw I used for sleeping. Each night Henry returned and replenished my food and water and exchanged my sanitation bucket. He walked with me up and down the length of the log pile to exercise my leg. He talked quietly to me during these walking sessions. He told me what progress he was making with the Underground. During the day, I did sit-ups and push-ups, but my knee remained stubbornly rigid and painful.

During my confinement of several weeks, I often saw a Dutch farmer and his children going to work in the nearby field. Sometimes I watched the German soldiers going through maneuvers. I watched them as they charged at each other, responded to orders, and sneaked along through the trees. Once during practice, a soldier ran up to the logs and thrust his bayonet forward. It scared me and I drew back in alarm, but the point stuck into one of the logs and the young soldier struggled a few seconds to remove it. I smothered a nervous giggle.

One evening towards the end of the second week, Henry crawled into the hiding place and we talked in low tones about the future.

"There are two places you can go: one, a group of English and Canadians who escaped after the battles of Arnhem and Nijmegen. They are hiding on farms that are near each other."

"Are they just hiding there, or planning some way to get back to the Allies?" I asked.

"A system of the British Army smuggles a small group of five or six at a time back to England."

"How long would it take to get me back?"

"I do not know that. They are taken out in the order they came in. There are many."

"And the other place?" I asked.

"You can join the Underground. There is a farm where already is an American and an Englishman. You would have a chance to fight, if you wish."

"I choose the second place. I want to do something, Henry, not just hide waiting for the war to end," I decided.

"Good. Soon we will move you from here — when it is the right time." Henry left me.

One morning just before daybreak, Henry came to my log hideout. He brought blue denim coveralls, an overcoat, a pair of shoes that fit and a bicycle. He also brought what was needed so I could shave.

"You must learn a few Dutch words to be spoken to the next man so he will know you," Henry said, as he watched me remove an accumulation of black beard. "Repeat after me. *Een verbrande paal dat eens eencedeelte van een boom was is altijd zielig omte zien.*"

I struggled with the words then repeated them again and again, trying to perfect my pronunciation. When I could speak the words to the ranger's satisfaction, he said, "He will answer in English, 'God save the King.' He will be waiting for you beside a burned fence post."

I practiced the words to myself while we walked across the field. I pushed the bicycle. We stopped at the canal, and Henry told me to repeat the words again. I did.

"What do the words mean?' I asked.

"Let me see." He scratched his chin. "A... A... burned post that was a tree is always very sad to see."

"You're a poet," I laughed.

"It was not my doing." He smiled, then pointed down the road. "You go that way. When you reach the crossroads, turn left. Talk to no one but the man you are supposed to talk to. Remember, he will be standing beside a burned fence post."

I gave the older man a hug. "I will never forget you or what you've done for me."

The big man hugged me in return. "Goodbye, God be with you!"

I found it hard to swallow. I watched Henry wave and stride off across the field. I pushed the bicycle across the canal and rode off down the road alone.

About thirty minutes later, I spotted a man, dressed entirely in black, standing beside a burned post, I stopped.

"*Een verbrande paal....*"

"God save the King!" the man interrupted me, and shook my hand enthusiastically. I winced as my shoulder complained. "I am called *Zwarte Jan* — Black John. I am leader of the Underground unit in my area," he added proudly. "You are Bobby." It was a statement and from that time on, he has always called me 'Bobby'. He retrieved a bicycle from behind the fence.

"Come, we have two hours of riding. I will lead, you follow behind me. Speak to no one." I nodded, understanding Jan's very heavy accent with difficulty.

We passed German soldiers and a lot of Dutch citizens. Once, we passed a little railroad station where there were four or five Germans with baggage. I figured they were soldiers going on leave.

We rode until about noon and stopped at a place that reminded me a little of a chicken farm in Petaluma, California. There was a hatchery setup and pens. We went in the back of this place and entered a barn. There were two or three fellows in there working on Bren guns and Sten guns, and they had parts spread all over the place. There were also several pistols. I looked around and saw that there was a small arsenal of arms hanging on the walls. They fed us and about a half hour later, we took off again. We stopped at two more farms along the way with the same set up. I could not see that anyone guarded these places or that any other precautionary measures were taken.

We made one more stop for lunch. They asked me what I would like to eat, and I answered that I would like cheese — white cheese. They had some cheese, and I kept wanting more. I thought there was cheese all over the place. I guess I ate about all they had. I learned later that the Germans had taken most of their cheese back into Germany. These people evidently had some cheese stashed and I must have eaten their whole supply!

Bobby's Story

After that, we rode steadily without stopping for awhile, then Jan turned up the driveway leading to a large farmhouse. We leaned our bicycles against a tree and walked to the door.

"This is Somsenhuis. It is the farm of the Prinzen family. They will keep you safe, and you can join the Underground in a few days when you have rested."

Before Jan could knock on the door, it opened and we were ushered in by Papa and Moeder Prinzen.

• • • • •

The Prinzen Family, c.1945

Chapter 7

Life at Somsenhuis

The room was quiet. Little Benny had fallen asleep and little Anna was close to sleeping, too. Papa picked up Benny while Moeder picked up Anna and they took them off to bed.

"Well, it is late," said Frank. "Perhaps we should all retire so that this hard-working family can get some rest." The rest of the Prinzen family protested. They wanted to hear more.

"There is no more to the story," Bob said, "We will see you tomorrow." And at that, all five of us rose and moved out to our hiding place in the hay where we prepared for sleep.

"I'm about talked out, the way my voice sounds," Bob said.

"There is a postscript to your story, though," Frank smiled. "Something you would appreciate, I'm sure. A day or two before you came down in your parachute, the Burgermeister [the German-appointed mayor] of the little town near where you landed was killed when he was driving in his car one day. He was shot up by some low flying British or American fighters. On the day you were shot down, he was being carried to his last resting place and his pall bearers had just got his coffin into the cemetery when your plane came roaring down into the cemetery. They had to drop this guy's coffin and run for it. This was a huge joke in the district, for this wretched Quisling was being pursued even to his grave!"

We all laughed at the story and felt better for it.

Papa was very capable. My mother used to say, 'Necessity is the mother of invention.' Papa was that kind of capable. One morning, he was making willow baskets. There were willow bushes growing in a drainage ditch in back of the farm. He had come back with armsful of these willow branches and started weaving a basket for carrying clothes and other things. He did a very neat job. They lacked so much they had to use everything they had because so many things were not available to buy.

Life at Somsenhuis

Papa had three brothers who lived nearby. One was a tailor and one had a store. From this store, many things they had hidden were made available to the farm to help out. Moeder also had three brothers, one was in the trucking business, and the other two were farmers, both living close to her parents, about one-eighth of a mile down the road.

Other than Bob learning to milk cows, the rest of us cut wood in a shed where no one could come upon us easily and see us. In the evening, we took turns peeling potatoes. Since there were so many people to feed, there were a lot of potatoes to peel.

Lots of times, the evening meal consisted of a cooked oatmeal-type of pudding. I learned to like it. The Dutch members called it something that sounded like 'Poc'. With that and a piece of bread and with something hot to drink, we ate very well.

One evening as we were eating, I took my knife and after getting some butter to put on my bread, I began trying to spread the butter. Because the weather was so cold, the butter was pretty hard. My knife broke. Papa Prinzen, obviously irritated, lectured me on how to spread butter with a knife. It was all in Dutch, of course, but I knew I was being reprimanded. I was both ashamed and sorry.

There was a young man, the son of a minister, who helped around the farm sometimes. He had a crush on Truida. She, apparently, was not so interested. Two of Truida's younger sisters tried to keep him from her whenever they could, but he was pretty determined. One day, they found him in Truida's bedroom, although she was not there at the time. Frank found out about it, picked him up by his collar, took him out and found a bit of hard, cement floor where he unceremoniously dropped him. There was no further problem.

Early one evening, some of us were milling around out in the dell in the barn and Truida came out and we were kind of teasing her, and Ted was teasing more than the rest of us. Suddenly, she took hold of him and hurled him into the cattle feeding bin. We all laughed, including Ted. We did a lot of teasing with the family and they teased back. I know it was one of the things that made us so close, even after we left their farm.

Most of the week our downstairs activities were in the kitchen. It was only on Sunday we gathered in the living room, or parlor. There was a fire in the fireplace and it was a treat to go in there each week.

One morning, Papa was going into the creamery at Aalten. He asked if we wanted anything from the creamery.

"Yes!" we almost said at once. "Bring us some buttermilk." So when he returned, he brought two and a half gallons of buttermilk. It tasted so good. We were fortunate because we were treated to something special — sometimes he brought us honey, cheese, and such, and this helped us get through some of the days. The family canned a lot of fruit during the summer so they had cherries and some pears. They were so good. The Prinzens always came through with some kind of meat, and the liverwurst we particularly liked. It was just delicious spread on some bread and butter. We often made a hearty meal out of that.

One day when I was peeling potatoes, I sliced off a piece of raw potato and ate it.

"You lika?" I was asked.

"Yea, that's *mui*." I was caught a few times doing the same thing with carrots.

During the cold winter nights when the stars were out and the moon was pretty bright, we went skating out where there was ice formed on the shallow lake in the field — not too deep — and we would go out there and some of us would ice skate and have fun and exercise.

All members of the family had their own chores to do. Even the smallest, who acted as a kind of watchdog. John, the fourth son, was the one who went after the bread and he got it at two different mills (*molen*). He carried food ration stamps that the Underground had stolen from somewhere, and he had money the Underground had stolen out of one of the banks rather than let it get into Nazi hands. John went to two different mills so that he would not raise suspicion as to why he was buying so much bread.

Marinus, the fifth son, made the cigars, and Hermein, the second daughter, made beds and helped her sister Truida and her mother wash and clean the house. Papa would generally wash dishes in the evening, sometimes with our help. He wanted to be sure they were thoroughly rinsed to make sure everyone stayed well.

Derk, the second son, was the one who did most of the farm work, plowing, planting and working with the horse. He did farm chores and saw that the younger boys did theirs. To me he looked a lot like King Edward VII.

Papa was an amazing gentleman. He almost had ESP. He seemed to be at the right spot at the time he was needed. When a soldier came to the house and knocked on the door, he was always there to distract. He handled several incidents like that magnificently.

This farm had chickens and cows, about fifteen pigs and one horse that pulled the cultivator used on the farm, and pulled the carriage which was used for special occasions. They had a wagon and several bicycles. He also understood how easily young people could get carried away, and was always there to keep order.

One day several members of the Underground came to the house with Jan Ket and they were very angry.

"Why did the Tommies strafe my doctor friend?" Jan demanded.

Frank tried to explain that so close to the border a pilot could not be sure where he was exactly. However, we found out later that the Germans had actually shot the doctor because they were suspicious that he was working for the Underground. They shot him and then let the word out that it was done by the Tommies. There were thousands of Dutch people who were executed for suspicion of Underground activities or listening to a radio.

There was another gentleman around the farm who sometimes worked for the family: Ben te Brink, an Underground member. He wore leather puttees around his pant legs. He always had a roll-your-own cigarette in his mouth as he worked and moved about. He drove a team and wagon for various farm tasks and Underground activities.

Willum (*met de bril*), meaning 'William with the glasses', also worked around the farm and was another *onderduiker* (Underground member). He told me one day he had read a book about Coloma, California, where a murder was committed and gold was discovered.

"That was a quite common thing to have happen at that time and place," I answered. "As a matter of fact, my home is very close to Coloma." He was surprised that I lived so close to the place he had read about.

Papa would tease us sometimes. He would come out to where we were and ask us things like, "Would you boys like some ice cream?" Of course we became very excited and said, "*Ja! Ja!* You have some ice cream?"

"No," he would say, "We would like some too!"

Sometimes he teased us when we were still around the table and had finished our evening meal.

"Who wants to sleep *met mijn vrouw* tonight?" Papa would ask.

We knew he was kidding us, but we played it through. We all jumped up shouting, "Me! Me!" and we would vie for the honor of taking Moeder's arm as though to escort her off to the bedroom. Of course, we went only two or three steps, Moeder giggling all the while. They were a fine and loving family and they all did their best to keep us from being too homesick. Most of the time they succeeded.

They were also true Christians. One of the ways they showed their devotion to their beliefs was hiding us and caring for us at great risk to themselves. Before each meal, Papa said Grace and read a few verses from the Bible.

Jan Ket did everything he could to keep us safe, too, and busy. He not only kept us busy with as much Underground work as we could safely do, but he sometimes took one of us into town to visit with people he trusted, not only to show them that his work was important, but to give one of us an outing, a change of scene so to speak.

When he was visiting Somsenhuis, it was often in the daytime. He had already instructed us to be aware of a code whistle in case of danger. The tune was usually the familiar 'Mary Had a Little Lamb'. The code was used quite a lot and we were frightened often.

One night when an Underground member, I believe it was Co Hettinga, was staying with us up in the hiding place, he told us that Jan Ket had been arrested three times by the Gestapo. He escaped each time and told us about one of the escapes.

Jan and a companion were arrested at the same time. Their hands were tied behind their backs and they were put into a canvas-covered truck. Two German guards got in the back with them. The two prisoners knew they were headed for Gestapo Headquarters to be 'interrogated'. In other words — shot!

The two German guards seated opposite them were each holding Mausers. They continually taunted the frightened prisoners while playfully fingering their rifle triggers.

Life at Somsenhuis

"Interrogation is nothing," said one soldier with false sincerity, and nudged his companion. They both exploded with laughter.

Under cover of the dimness inside the canopied space and the truck's bouncing, the two partisans were working feverishly. They had slipped their bound hands outside between the sideboard and canvas and with maximum stretching had succeeded in unfastening the rope that lashed down the canopy.

For some reason, the truck slowed to a stop. The guards looked out to see why. That is when the prisoners leaped up, flung themselves backward hard against the canvas, fell through the opening, landed rolling, and were on their feet and running before their surprised tormentors reacted.

Another time Jan was imprisoned, he was deposited on the second floor in a room with one window. All was cement surface outside, but Jan, determined to stay alive, found a way to open the window. He jumped from the second story onto the cement in a roll and escaped.

The Dutch Underground organization was the unofficial expeditor of Holland's private commerce. Businessmen and farmers were made to pay a large part of their production to the Germans. The people kept back and hid as much as they were able. Jan Ket's unit worked as coordinators. At night they would take grain from the farmer to the miller for flour, or a cowhide to the shoemaker. His pay was in meat, flour, or some other commodity that was scarce in the town.

The British dropped guns and dynamite in plastique form. If the opportunity arose, the Underground did what damage they could to hinder the Germans' movements. Each delay was a gain for the Allies and a booster for Dutch moral.

Ted went to mass a few times with Co who was also Catholic and an active member of the Underground. One time when he returned he told us what happened.

"We found a suitable place to sit after lighting candles, and when I was in prayer, I realized that two German soldiers had come in and sat down beside me. I'm afraid I couldn't concentrate on the prayer I was into — it sort of changed to, 'God keep me safe!'"

One night, Bobby went into town with Jan Ket, on one of his visits. It was absolutely imperative that they be off the streets and out of town before curfew, which was eight o'clock. Persons caught out after curfew were often shot — no questions asked.

On the way out of town, Bob got his bicycle front wheel caught in the trolley tracks and fell. His companions stopped and looked back to see Bobby being helped to his feet and back onto his bicycle by two German soldiers with flashlights. Bobby kept telling them "*Danka! Danka!*" in his good old American Dutch. No one seemed the wiser. They went riding on down the street laughing their heads off at the situation.

Frank Dell went to town with Jan Ket one time and while they were in the living room visiting Jan's friends, a German officer who was billeted there came in to go to his room upstairs. The officer greeted everyone on his way up to his room and a mumbled response was returned. The officer continued on his way up the stairs apparently unaware of exactly who was sitting there. Frank said he found he had been holding his breath because he suddenly felt the need to breathe.

Of course, we all wore civilian clothes over our uniforms, even while in the Prinzen home. Wherever we went, we dressed that way.

Joe Davis and I never went on these jaunts into town since both of us were married with families at home and we did not want to take the risk. Neither did we enter into the acts of sabotage for the same reason.

Chapter 8

Christmas and the New Year

"Does anyone happen to know what day this is?" Frank suddenly asked one evening when we were standing outside the barn door watching the clear starry night.

"Let's see, it must be about the twenty-second or twenty-third of December," Joe answered.

"That's right, it's the twenty-third," Ted said, "I've been making little marks on the wall in the hiding room. I wasn't sure I should bring it up under the circumstances."

"On the contrary," Frank said, and added, "Haven't you noticed a little bit more excitement in the house lately? More people coming and going?"

"But we have nothing to give them," I said.

"Yes, we do, Owen," Bob put in, "We can give them love, cooperation, laughter, and appreciation."

"That won't be hard to do," Joe sighed, "But it would be nice if we could give them something wrapped up in green with red ribbon."

"They usually celebrate their St. Nicholas on the sixth of December, but this year they decided for our sakes — and only Joe, Bob and I were here then — to wait until the twenty-fifth," said Frank.

We went to our hiding place wishing we could do something special for the Prinzen family. Soon we settled down to sleep.

The next day about mid-morning, the children came in with a basket loaded with shiny aluminum strips. These strips (chaff) were dropped by the Allied bombers as they neared the bomb run of their targets. This caused the anti-aircraft radar to track the chaff instead of the bombers, particularly effective in overcast conditions.

Those children brought in this bright chaff which was almost like Christmas tree icicles, only a bit wider. They took it in the house where we joined the family and we all decorated the mantle, the window sills, and over the doorways. They had also cut some greenery which we put around the room in various places. It looked very homey.

That night, Christmas Eve, it was cold, clear, and the stars were very bright. There were stripes of light from the searchlights and we could hear the booming of war in the distance.

"Look at those stars!" I said, "They seem to light up the whole sky. Stars and stripes, stars and stripes — I think I'm getting a little homesick."

"It is because of Christmas," Frank said quietly. "It's normal for one to think about home at this time. Shall we join the family?"

"What about the family, Frank?" Bob asked, "Black Jan keeps telling us the front is moving this way. Pretty soon we're going to be overrun by retreating German soldiers. They could get pretty mean. I know I've got someplace to hide but what about the family if the Germans somehow find out what they've been doing?"

In listening to our battery-powered radio, we knew that the front was in the Ardennes area [where the American Army was fighting in the Battle of the Bulge, 200 miles away, on the Franco-Belgian border].

"After Christmas Day, we will work out something. Right now, I suggest we all join in what fun we can have, especially for the children," answered Frank as they went through the door into the warm kitchen. "Black Jan is coming tomorrow."

"Black Jan is coming on Christmas Day?" asked Ted. He rubbed his arms up and down to help warm them.

"Yes," Frank answered. He unwound a scarf from his neck. "He told me he has invited a *Dominee* Klijn to come and give us all Christmas services," he continued. "He'll have to smuggle him through in broad daylight, but Jan is very clever. He said he would be here, so I am certain he will."

We spent the remainder of the evening playing with the children. The three women had finished their work and had disappeared to some other part of the house. Papa sat by the *kachel*, warming his sock-clad feet. Everyone in the room was relaxed. We all knew that on this night there were Underground members guarding the house. Tonight no one feared that the door would suddenly be opened by a curious or hungry soldier.

The next morning at the breakfast table, each of us five had a gift-wrapped little package at the side of our plates. After Grace, Papa indicated

Christmas and the New Year

that we should open them as they were from the family to us. Unwrapping the gifts, which were all alike, we found a comb, hand-made from plexiglass of downed aircraft. The teeth were cut with a file saw. We each received some Dutch cigars as well. We were all very surprised and moved. After thanking the Prinzen family, we ate our breakfast and as quickly as possible cleared away all the signs of breakfast. Then we moved into the parlor.

When Jan Ket and *Dominee* Klijn arrived at the farmhouse, the Reverend greeted everyone in the room. There were the twelve Prinzens, five airmen and several members of the Resistance. When asked if he had any trouble in getting to the farm, this is what he said:

"Early this morning before it was light, Jan led me through the German lines by way of a labyrinth of sandy roads and narrow lanes. As you can see, we both wore black. Suddenly, we were facing a guard with a Sten gun," he continued. "Black Jan spoke one word softly and the guard lowered his gun. They were comrades in arms, you see. Behind the guard we could see the dark outlines of this farmhouse rising up against the sky."

Truida brought the two men mugs of hot ersatz with fresh milk and sweetener. Hermein offered sweet cakes baked the day before. When they felt warm inside as well as outside the service began at once. *Dominee* Klijn was scheduled to be at his own church at the regular time so could not stay for an indefinite period.

A Resistance worker was at the organ. The Reverend spoke to him briefly and then he opened his Bible.

The Gospel of St. Luke was read in that simple kitchen with an international circle of listeners who had gathered to hear the familiar words. The *Dominee* spoke first in Dutch, then in English. Listening to the old Christmas message brought to us in our own language was very moving. Some of us were from as far away as California. It was the universal message: A Savior was born of the house of David, the Lord Messiah. All of us who heard this message were fighting for peace on earth and understood: 'Glory to God in high heaven and peace on earth for men whom he favors!'

By some miracle, the Underground had located a few English hymn books so the Christmas carols were sung together in both languages: 'Honor to God', 'Hark the Herald Angels Sing', and the much loved

'Silent Night, Holy Night'. The organist played a Christmas solo, and the quiet in the room was wonderful. He was wearing a large mustache as a disguise since he was forever on the move throughout Holland giving lectures and instruction to recruited Resistance members.

Joe gazed at the big stove, the red glow from the fire reflected on his face. Bob, usually restless, was quiet. My eyes were damp as I watched the four-year-old whose eyes were big and his body still. I was thinking of my own wife and baby girl at home. Frank sat straight, but relaxed, with eyes closed. Though we fought under different flags, we were united in our desire for freedom for all, especially for this Dutch family. In addition, there was our bold Underground commander, Jan, who had faced death several times, and other Resistance workers who had been in the Dutch Navy and the Dutch Army.

I will never forget that Christmas. I have never been so moved as on that day.

The next day we went back to helping the Underground. In addition, we helped the family in any way we could. One important way was to stay out of sight as much as possible so that there would be no sad disasters. In the meantime, we kept track of the war by our little battery radio which we only turned on for the news — not for entertainment. Batteries were difficult to find. This radio was powered by an automobile battery.

Henk van t'Lam, second-in-command in the Underground, had a sister, Kokkie. She actively worked in the Underground. Many young women did. Women could often do things that the men could not do, and so cleverly that there was no suspicion involved. However, Kokkie had a brush with the soldiers. She was thrown in jail for a few days, but then she was released.

She often came to the farm for visits. She and her girl-friend, Nonie, sister to the local doctor, and Truida, organized a celebration for New Year's Eve. The five of us did not make any particular plans, and we did not know about the plans in the making by these three young women, Papa, and Jan Ket.

From somewhere (they did not explain) they had acquired two barrels of schnapps. These were happily received and we had a party. Jan Ket was there as well as his second-in-command and a few of the Resistance

Christmas and the New Year

workers. It wasn't long before the night grew late and the schnapps level in the barrels descended. Truida was having such a good time serving the drink, and drinking it herself, she eventually had the liquid running down her arms. Careful not to waste anything, she licked it off her arms and laughed about it. Many of the rest of us had our hands wet with it.

We all knew Truida thought a lot of Frank. He did not take advantage of it, however, but always treated her with friendliness and respect. During this New Year's Eve celebration, he had to be especially careful of drawing the fine line between his utter respect for her and making sure that she did not draw conclusions that were wrong. In any event, there was no possibility of a serious development since Papa was always alert to every event on the farm.

We teased Frank later. We asked him what he would do if, after the war, he found her on his doorstep. Always the gentleman, he replied that he did not know. He thought he would just wait and see.

One evening after Christmas week, we were up in our hiding place when we heard quite a commotion in the cow stanchion. We all came down the ladder to see what all the noise was about. Several members of the family were helping to tie a rope to the back legs of the calf which was protruding from the birth canal. We watched as they gently tugged at the calf's legs to assist in the delivery. Cows never got out of the stanchions during the winter so have little or no exercise to keep the muscles strong that they needed to use for unassisted birthing. During this episode, Truida got salt to reduce the swelling. I understand that sugar is better, but sugar was very hard to come by in this war-torn land.

Chapter 9

Plans

After New Year's day, we continued our work with the Underground, but then one morning about the middle of January, we watched, fascinated, as the Prinzen family made liverwurst and bloodwurst sausage. When the farmers butchered hogs, they used every possible part of the animals. In making the sausage, they cleaned the intestines by washing them, washing them over and over, inside and out. They even used a brush. This scrubbed lining was used for the casings for the sausages. Moeder's mother came from down the road and the two German soldiers from Alsace-Lorraine who had deserted came to help as well, because one of them had been a butcher in civilian life. They would fill these casings with the sausage mix and periodically cut the lining so that there was a small length beyond the filling. Each sausage was then tied at both ends. I had never seen this done before.

Jan Ket's wife, Emmy, came to the Prinzen farm sometimes on visits. She was a very pretty lady. Their young son, Benny Ket, rode in a basket behind her on the bicycle. Emmy was born in Germany and she had a brother in the German Army who was always trying to get Jan to join the German Army. Obviously, he did not know about Jan's Underground activities.

For that reason, and many others, when Jan wanted to see Emmy, he had to slip in a back window — if he could get her attention long enough to do this. Emmy hid Allied flyers also and there was always the chance of being watched. It was all very touchy.

Soon after New Year's, the Underground thought we could be taken by boat down the river through the enemy lines. They had done this before by this method. Their plans were made and we held an elaborate farewell dinner. As we were toasting our journey, we heard the guns from the front sounding exceptionally loud. We waited until late that night for the Dutchmen to come for us. While we were waiting, the guns kept

Plans

pounding. Our guide finally arrived and sorrowfully told us that the Canadian Artillery barrage had shot up our boat.

The Underground began scheming for some other way to get us out. Two German generals had an airplane known as a Fieseler Storch. These two generals, Model and Student, were involved in organizing the defense at Arnhem. They were responsible for the northern end of the so-called 'West World'. They kept their airplane in a field close by. I believe it was Co Hettinga who went out on the field and talked to the mechanic who, every morning, pre-flighted this airplane.

This mechanic would taxi it down to one end of the field and then taxi it back during the pre-flight. One of the boys figured they could get in there and grab the ground crew of the plane and we could go ahead, then, and warm up the plane. When we taxied to the other end of the field for take-off, this would cause no excitement among the Germans because it was the usual procedure in the mornings. We could get the thing off the ground and get away. Co found out that it was kept fully fueled so we thought this was just a great way to get home — by flying a German general's plane!

In the meantime, Black Jan wanted to bomb the headquarters of these two generals while they were in the building. That would be a serious move against the German cause. So Jan Ket got our radio operator to send a message on to London to give them coordinates of the particular house that was the Germans' headquarters. You see, it was better for everyone's safety if the aircraft of the Germans' enemies could do the sabotage rather than the Underground, in some cases because then there would not be the same reprisals as a result.

The message was received in London, but while we were working out the details of stealing the plane, the generals took the airplane and flew off. A day or two later, over came these rocket-firing Typhoons. They put a lot of rockets into this building, and they also put a few rockets into the building next door. The building next door was the location of our radio transmitter. So, the generals were not in the building at the time, and the Underground lost a radio transmitter, and we lost our chance to steal the generals' plane!

One day, there was the first snow on the ground. At least the temperature was a little warmer, but it was harder to get around at night. At any rate, we still went to 'de Bark' to help. One of the ways we helped from the beginning was to teach some of the Dutchmen about Sten guns and Bren guns — to get them familiar with the advantages of hand grenades, and the dangers as well. The pistols were less familiar to the Resistance members than rifles. As for the bazookas, they did not know much about them at all. After a few weeks they caught on — how to load and unload any of the firearms, how to fire them accurately, and how to take care of them and themselves. There were a few accidents as I have already related, but no one was really hurt, for which we all felt lucky.

Right after the first week of February, Frank began to talk in a very strange way. He ate, he slept, he took care of his personal needs, but his speech was garbled. He made no sense at all. He seemed to know he was ill so he took to the sleeping area. He stayed there most of the time for about two weeks.

Then the snow began to fall and this was both good and bad. The good part was that we were tramping out in not quite so terrible cold, and we could see better at night. The bad part, we could be seen more easily. I suppose we could have dragged a tree branch behind us to cover our tracks, but we didn't. We took our chances because the tracks on the trail were already established. So the important work of the Underground continued regardless of the snow and an occasional snow storm that made visibility difficult.

Now it was the end of the third week of February. It was evening and Frank's first day down out of the hayloft. The door opened and Jan Ket entered followed by another man we did not know. He introduced him to Papa and Moeder Prinzen first, and then to us. His name was Jim Strickland, from Australia. So another Allied country was represented in Somsenhuis.

Jim had walked for a very long way out of Germany with only a few rest stops, and was truly tired. He was given food and then we showed him our hiding place. He gratefully sank down on the thick layer of straw and was probably asleep before we left him. As we were descending the loft, I noticed that his shoes were worn thin and partly in tatters.

We went back to the kitchen where Jan was talking in low tones to Papa and Moeder. As we came in Jan turned to us.

Plans

"He has done a lot of walking and has come a long way. He is still fit, but very tired," Jan said, "When he is rested, he will probably feel fine."

The next day Frank took a bicycle ride with Co Hettinga on Underground business and they were gone for about three days. This place was about five miles away and we did not think that Frank was quite strong enough, but he went anyway.

In the next twenty-four hours, Jim slept most of the time. When he came down the ladder and Truida asked if he was hungry, he definitely was. We gathered around the kitchen and watched while he ate and when he was finished, I asked, "Do you feel up to telling us your story from the time you left your airplane until you arrived here?"

"Of course!" Jim replied, "If you chaps will tell me yours."

The evening was young so we told him about ourselves, and then he began his story, beginning with his training in Australia.

Chapter 10

Jim's Story

• • •

It was early in 1942, when I joined the Royal Australian Air Force. I went through training schools in Australia — in Victoria, in New South Wales at Parks, for wireless training, and at gunnery school in Port Pirie in South Australia. I graduated a sergeant wireless operator and received orders for overseas duty.

I left with other Australian troops at Brisbane and traveled by an American ship across the Pacific to San Francisco. From there, we were taken by troop train across the United States to Boston and had a period of six weeks at Camp Miles Standish.

We then sailed on the *Queen Elizabeth* from New York, arriving four or five days later at Greenock, Scotland. We were taken by troop train to Brighton in the south of England, where we spent a few days on leave before being allocated to our various training schools. I was sent to a wireless school near Carnarvon in Northern Wales. After that, we went to Richfield in the Midlands where we were crewed up with the boys who completed a bomber crew. We had a period of training and we were converted from a twin-engine Wellington aircraft to four-engine bombers. We eventually went on to a squadron near Lincoln. This was one of two Australian squadrons on this particular station.

My first assigned pilot went off with an experienced pilot on orientation, we called it a 'second dicky' trip, and he was lost with that bomber crew. It was a raid over the Ruhr Valley area.

My crew members and I were most anxious to stay together because we had developed a great camaraderie and we were friendly with Flight Lieutenant Boyle who was coming back for his second tour of operations and was looking for an Australian crew. We did a Lancaster finishing school with him and he took us back on to Squadron number 467. We did twenty-five operational flights over Germany with Flight Lt. Boyle. He was then transferred from active duty because this completed a second tour of operations for him.

The powers-that-be decided it was a good idea to keep our crew together, so we became a much closer-knit crew under Wing Commander Douglas who had come out of another Australian Squadron, number 460. We operated with Wing Commander Douglas from about October 1944 until the 7th of February 1945.

On that date, we were involved in a bombing attack on the Dortmund-Ems Canal. This was my 27th mission. We were due over the target about midnight. We attacked the target successfully without any difficulty, but our gunners reported to the pilot that they could see other bombers were being attacked and there was fighter activity in the area.

"'Sir!" Tom, the rear gunner, reported, "Some of the other kites [aircraft] are hit and there are a great lot of fighters around."

"'Steady!" the Commander's voice was soothing. "Our engines are humming along nicely."

Hearing those words, I thought, well, maybe it wasn't our time yet, so I switched off the intercom and nervously lit a cigarette, inhaling deeply. We were flying back towards England doing a banking search because of this fighter activity when suddenly the aircraft jolted severely. I quickly switched on the intercom. The pilot was calling, "Bail out. Bail out!"

The others of the crew heard it before I did so my reaction was to leave the aircraft as quickly as possible. I grabbed my chest-type 'chute, clipped it to my chest harness and made my way to the rear escape hatch. When I reached it, my mid-upper gunner was spread-eagled over the hatch. He had been hit and was hesitant about bailing out. I persuaded him to abandon ship. I was getting a little excited, you see, so I physically helped him to make up his mind. He subsequently left the aircraft and I quickly followed him out.

I was swishing through the black void. All was deadly quiet. Suddenly, there was a tremendous jerk. I could feel the straps of the 'chute pulling very tightly across my thighs, and my legs felt they were in very strong vises. I stretched my arms up and relieved some of the pressure by pulling myself up by the shroud lines above me. When I jumped from the aircraft, it was about 8,000 feet altitude.

As I floated through the clouds, it was a rather eerie sensation. It was a very dark night. Suddenly, I heard a voice calling out, "Can you hear me?" I recognized the voice of the Canadian navigator who had traveled with us on this particular mission as a second navigator.

I called back to him, but we did not have any further conversation. I don't know whether he heard me or not because I was drifting in a thick cloud. I was not aware of the aircraft. A moment or two before this, I had seen it disappear in the distance looking very much like a great ball of fire.

I looked down and saw something that looked like a large mound of blackness rushing towards me and I thought, 'Well, this is the ground coming up, I'd better get prepared to hit it.' I remembered during training the instructor saying, 'The safest way to land is keep your knees together.' All of a sudden, 'Bonk!' I was on the ground. I had landed in a bank of soft soil. I was not hurt in any way so I collected myself and rolled up my parachute and dug a hole in the soft earth and buried it. Then I decided to get out of the area as quickly as possible.

In the distance, I saw some dim lights through the black night that I judged to be about two hundred yards away. I decided to go in another direction which I presumed to be West. I was uncertain of my position. In fact, I was not sure I was in Germany. We had been flying in a westerly direction making for the Dutch border. I heard the sounds of a steam train about four or five hundred yards from where I landed. I went in the direction of the sound to find the railroad tracks. I found the tracks and climbed up a steep bank, then surveyed the countryside. I couldn't see too much, so decided to follow the railroad line for awhile and hoped I would come upon a road. The advice we received during our training was, 'Walk only during the night.' This was my plan.

I had walked about a half mile when I came upon a roadway. I saw no activity so decided to follow this road. I soon came upon a stand like dairy farmers use to put their cans of milk on until they are picked up in the morning. Jolly good! I had a good drink of milk. Then as a gesture to help the war effort, I tipped the rest of milk from all the cans onto the road. After this bit of mischief, I felt a great sense of satisfaction!

A bit further, I came to a village. I guessed it to be about two o'clock in the morning. At my approach to the village, I could hear some people singing in a house. I stealthily moved right through the middle of the village then continued along the road for some hours.

When the sky began to get light, I looked for a likely spot along the road to hide for the day. I climbed a fence and walked into a wooded area. There was a depression in the ground well hidden by some bushes. I sat there for that day. I studied the map I had and it didn't make a lot of sense to me because I didn't know where I was anyway. I sucked at a number of concentrated food tablets from my escape kit. There was plenty of water available. I filled my water bottle and just sat there.

'You know this is a funny sort of business. You are the only person in the world that knows that you're alive!' I thought. 'I wonder if my family back home have been told I'm missing in action. If they only knew that I'm not a captive — not yet anyway.' There were a few other things that went through my mind — my two sisters at home in Australia were having birthdays this month. 'Well, jolly good luck to them! There they are having parties and I can't even send them best wishes.'

At nightfall I set off again across country. By this time, I'd had a look at my compass that was concealed in one of the buttons of my tunic. I continued in a westerly direction. At least it would take me closer to England.

The weather was cold and there was sleet falling. I was cold and stiff after sitting all day behind the bushes. I decided no more of that. From then on, I would keep on walking while I was awake and find a place to sleep when I got tired.

Three days after I had been shot down, I was pretty weary and wet through. So, the dark blue jumper I was wearing under my tunic, I changed to wearing over my tunic. I then looked more like the people I saw. I broke off a branch of a tree to carry over my shoulder to blend in even more thoroughly. I wanted to look like a person with a job or someone who was gathering wood for the heating stove.

My subterfuge must have worked because I soon passed a farmer with a horse and cart and he said something like, "Hru-m-p! Good morning!"

I answered with a similar 'hru-m-p!' and kept on walking.

On the fourth night, I was very tired and footsore. It was about an hour after nightfall, I needed to find shelter out of the sleet and cold. I saw a farmhouse and decided I would try to seek shelter. The wind was howling. It was a pretty miserable night. I could see a chink of light through the window and I knocked on the door. No one answered. I pounded on the door. Still no answer. Then I decided it was rather foolish to expect to be welcomed into a German household.

I left the farmhouse and made my way across country until I came to an outbuilding of another farmhouse. This building was used to store firewood. There was chopped firewood in a heap on the ground. I went in and made myself as comfortable as possible and soon fell asleep. In the early hours of the morning I heard a dog barking and I woke up, still half asleep. I shook the grogginess out of my head. I looked out the open door and saw a dog coming along the pathway followed by a man who looked to be middle-aged to elderly. I assumed he was German.

He came to the door, spoke to me, and pointed along the roadway. I didn't understand what he was saying. He pointed to me and then to the road. It was fairly clear. He wanted me to leave down the road. I figured the war would not last much longer and generally the populace would try to hand one over to the Gestapo.

"Gestapo," I said, and pointed down the road. He spoke to me again in German and I still didn't know what he was saying. I watched him walk away from me back towards a clump of trees, and he would occasionally stop, turn and look at me to see if I was following.

When we reached the roadway, there were a number of military vehicles passing, all filled with German soldiers. It seemed rather funny to me that he did not hail one of them and tell them about me. 'I've an Allied airman here,' he could have said, but he did not.

He went into a clump of trees and to a bike leaning against a tree. He took the bike and returned to the road walking along side of the bicycle about two or three hundred yards in front of me. He mounted his bike and rode slowly, still checking to see if I was following.

'I say, Old Boy,' I thought to myself, 'You're a bit of a nut to follow this chap along the road like you're doing,' so I jumped over a fence and ran away across the field. I noticed the old chap was crippled slightly. I saw him get off his bike and he immediately started yelling in a very loud voice. I ignored him. I kept running. Eventually, I hid and looked back at him from out my hiding place. I saw him ride off down the road toward what looked to me like a small town or village about a mile away. I never saw him again.

I continued on cross-country. It was raining and very cold. I found a cowshed and put in there for a few hours and even had some rest. While I considered my position, I kept a wary eye toward the village, but saw no activity. I did notice a couple of German soldiers on motorbikes, but it didn't appear they were searching for me so I continued on my way. I was in a pine forest.

I continued to walk in a westerly direction in the forest for the next three days, hiding among the trees for sleep when I got tired. I was feeling tired but fit. In the dark, while walking, I heard two people coming along the track from the opposite direction. I flattened myself against a tree and they went on by. I never knew if they were German soldiers or civilians. I continued on my way without further trouble.

I saw a town looming up and it looked to be a reasonable size. I was feeling fairly casual about the whole situation because I hadn't been caught, so I walked into this town which later I found out was Winterswijk. I approached the town unnoticed. A petrol pump by an old, ramshackle garage had a 'Texaco' name on it.

Something sort of clicked with me and made me think I wasn't in Germany, but I wasn't sure. I continued through the town passing several shops that mostly had dirty windows. I saw a 'Purcel Soap' sign and this rang a bell. I decided I was in Holland where they might use that brand of English soap.

As I walked along the street, I noticed quite a lot of troop activity. German soldiers were walking everywhere around town, tall elite-type troops. This was my first experience seeing the *Wehrmacht* at close range. I didn't say 'hello', but just walked quietly along, looking at the houses that were right along the foot path. In fact, I looked in a couple of windows and when I saw a photo on the mantle of a Dutch sailor wearing the traditional sailor-type hat with the orange pompom on top, I knew I was in Holland. I was told back in England to try to be picked up by the Dutch Underground. However, I had no idea how to make a contact.

I approached a store I thought might have people who would help me. I stood by the door. It was only a little shop, about fifteen by twenty feet with a little counter at the left of the doorway. I waited until there was no one in the shop and I opened the door, went in and stood at the counter.

A fellow in his mid-thirties or forties came to the counter and I started to try to make conversation with him. His face was a blank so I knew he did not understand me. Two younger men came into the shop and came up to the counter and I stood aside a little. The shop keeper made some remark to those two. One looked at me and laughed and said something. It appeared he was addressing me and laughed, so I stood there and said nothing. The two men walked out of the shop, and once again I tried to communicate with the shopkeeper. Again, his face was a blank. I could not tell if he was frightened or not.

"I'm an airman," I said to him, and gestured that I came down in a parachute by holding my hands up in the air and holding my arms out like the wings of an aircraft. He didn't seem impressed. Suddenly I remembered some coins in my pocket. I took them out and laid them on the counter and said, "England". He said nothing. A girl came from the rear of the shop and spoke to me in halting English. She looked to be about seventeen years of age.

Jim's Rescue

"Come quickly!" she said and opened up a little hatch in the counter. She walked me behind the shelving of the shop. The conversation that followed between her and another woman in the back of shop I could not understand, but they were very frightened. They were obviously aware I was an RAF member. In fact, they asked if I was RAF and I nodded my head 'yes'. I took out my escape map and spread it out on the table.

"Where am I?" I asked, pointing to the map. They pointed to Winterswijk. They asked if I had any food and I showed them my remaining supply of food tablets and water bottle. They buttered some thick slices of bread, and the girl spoke.

Jim's Story

"You must leave quickly."

"Where are the Tommies?" I asked.

"You go that way." She pointed down the road and I took off at a brisk pace in the direction she had pointed. I soon left the town behind, but it was obvious I was on the main road. No one seemed to be interested in me, however. That suited me just fine.

About a half hour later, two girls came along on push bikes. One of the girls was the one who spoke to me in the shop.

"Follow me," she said, and I walked off the road and we went up behind some bushes and trees.

"We can help you. You must go to Varsseveld." I wrote this down on a piece of paper, including a certain house I was to go to — number 27, I think. The girls conversed with me in halting English for a few minutes. One of the questions they asked me was, did I have a gun? I told them no.

They mounted their bikes and rode back toward town. Before they left, I found out it was about fifteen miles to Varsseveld. With the number of daylight hours I had left, I would have to hurry to get to that house before dark. After about two and a half hours it began to rain so I singled out a person that looked friendly and asked, "Varsseveld?" He looked at me with a blank expression. I repeated my question. He quickened his steps and walked away.

The rain got heavier and I decided I had had it. I saw a house off to the side of the road. There were no other houses around. 'I'll give it a try,' I thought. Maybe I'd be lucky.

I went up to the front door and banged on it. The door opened and there stood a woman silhouetted by the light from a long hallway.

"Let me in. I'm an Englander," I said. She closed the door in my face, but before it was completely closed, I stuck my foot in the way. As I did this, a couple of men came from the kitchen. They had heard the disturbance and came racing through the door and confronted me in the hallway. All the while I was calling out, "Englander! Englander!" They grabbed me and took me into the kitchen. I soon found that they were friendly and I calmed down.

The men indicated I should take off my clothes, so I took my reefer-neck [sweater] off, and my tunic. They indicated that I should sit down, so I did, and pulled my flying boots off and my socks that were wet through. There was a wonderful fire burning in the kitchen stove so I hung up my socks nearby. They gave me hot milk to drink. While I drank the milk there was a lively conversation going between the two men and the woman and two girls. I was particularly interested in the two young girls.

One came and sat beside me and put her arm around my shoulders and I thought, 'Well, that's a good idea and I'll have a bit of your shoulder too!' so I cuddled up to her. I thought this was great fun and I started to laugh and talked to the lot of them. I had a little gold kangaroo badge on my lapel of my uniform and one of the lasses showed a bit of interest in this and I handed it to her. She also saw the wooly tops to my flying boots so I tore them off and handed them to her. There was a bit of laughter that went on for a few minutes when something was said that sounded like, '*Ich schloppin wid me?*' Anyway, she indicated she wouldn't mind if I tucked up with her for the night!

I don't know whether it was her father or one of the men who said, "We've got to get him out of here." One of the men disappeared and about a half hour later, during which time I was still sitting comfortably cuddling with this girl, a tall fellow walked in the door.

"I am Barker," he said extending his hand.

"My name is Strickland." I stood up and shook his hand.

"Are you a pilot?"

"Yes," I answered.

"I must take you to another place," he said, so I began putting on my clothes, but I couldn't get my boots back on. My feet were badly swollen. A man got on either side of me and helped me out of the house, up a pathway for a hundred yards or so. We approached another house.

"Quiet! Do not speak!" One of the chaps whispered in my ear.

When they opened the door, I could see right into the kitchen. I briefly spotted two Germans sitting at the kitchen table and a chill went down my spine as the two men walked me to the right, on and up a flight of stairs into a bedroom with a great iron bedstead. I undressed and they put me to bed. I had no difficulty going to sleep.

Next morning, the door opened and a man asked in halting English, "How do you feel? We will bring a doctor to you today." He crossed over to the wardrobe, opened the doors, pulled out a battered suitcase from a pile of trash. He opened the suitcase and revealed a radio.

"We will listen to BBC," he said. So very quietly he turned it on — all the while he was softly laughing and joking. I guess I looked pretty miserable there in bed and he wanted to brighten up my sad life.

"There are soldiers in the courtyard below my window," and he opened the window and called remarks to them, at the same time saying obscene things, softly, that only I could hear. He waved to them and smiled and to me he said things like, "stupid Germans."

During the day, a doctor came and examined me.

"How do you feel?"

"My feet are tired and swollen."

"You seem to be in pretty fair physical condition. You might have to leave soon." The doctor left.

Later, a man came into my room and asked me questions.

"Where was your base?"

"I can't tell you any more than that my name is Strickland and my number 419231."

"I want to know what kind of aircraft you were flying. What squadron were you on?" he persisted.

I finally decided to break the rules a bit and so I spilled the beans and told him what he wanted to know.

"Where is the rest of your crew?" But I did not know.

"Can you ride a bicycle?"

"Yes."

"We will come with a bike tomorrow night. That will give your feet another day to rest."

The following night, he arrived with a bicycle and we set off along some bike tracks. He told me before we started that I must not speak.

We had only gone forward a few minutes when I fell off the bike. I was sitting on the ground trying to collect my wits. I couldn't hear my guide. He had disappeared in the darkness. Since I was not allowed to call, I whistled as though calling a dog a couple of times. Pretty soon he came back along the track and he said in a deep voice, "We will try again."

As I mounted my bike, he told me softly that the tracks are worn into a groove from long use. I must feel the front wheel and stick to the middle at the lowest point. That way I would stay on the path.

Before too long, we came to another house. They took me in. This house was right in the town of Varsseveld, across from the town hall. I was installed in a room at the front of the house. They told me I was not to go out of the room and if anyone came in, I wasn't to speak. Then the door closed.

I spent two or three days sitting in this room. There were curtains across the windows which looked directly out onto a footpath. I saw plenty of German soldiers walking around and I just sat there watching the people go by.

When it was time for a meal, I ate with the family. They tried to talk to me and I didn't understand one word. In my effort to talk back to them, my voice would get too loud and they would have to 'shush' me quiet again.

Instructions were that, except for Underground members and the family, I was deaf and dumb. I must not speak to anyone else, or at all if someone outside the family or Underground came in the house, particularly Germans who were likely to walk in without warning or a by-your-leave. They warned me that if someone did, I wasn't to panic, let a couple of minutes go by, then get up and quietly leave the room.

About the third morning at this place, I was sitting at the kitchen table eating my breakfast. The men had gone to work. A young German soldier, about twenty-two years old, walked into the room, said "Good morning," and I said nothing. We were sitting at this table about four feet long, me at one end and him at the other. He put his legs up on top of the table and looked at me. One of the females said something to him. She probably told him I was a 'nut' sitting there. As I had been instructed to do, I rose after a couple of minutes and left for my quarters. Apparently, he was not suspicious in any way. I, however, was shaking and covered with sweat when I sat down on my bed. The great pistol he carried was planted in my memory for a long time to come.

The next night, they took me to another place. I think it was near Aalten. They introduced me to a man whose name was Baker. He had a wife and a little boy about four years old.

They lived in what looked to be an old dairy building about twenty or thirty feet from this farmhouse. Their house had been bombed, so this dairy building was turned into a dwelling for them. The building was about fifteen feet by eight or nine feet, and there was a screened off part at one end for a bedroom for the young couple and a couch at the other end against the wall where I slept at night. I was there a few days. I was told not to go out in the daytime, but at night I went outside for a bit of exercise. One night when I went out, there was a lot of aerial activity and several Dutchmen were standing out there watching a couple of airplanes get shot up.

Each morning, the man went off to work and I was left there with the young wife and little boy. We started to try to communicate. I would point to a food item, she would say the Dutch word for it, and I supplied the English word. Before long we were carrying on a conversation of sorts and talked of many things, including sex.

"Are there a lot of nice girls in England to sleep with?" she asked, and that's how I spent my time, talking to her. About four days later, the Underground man came.

"I'm going to take you to another place where there are other British pilots," he said, which made me very pleased and excited and I looked forward to the next move.

"This will be great! I can meet someone else I can talk to," I said. I really believe they took so long to get me placed because German Intelligence was trying to break into their Underground network, so they probably looked upon me with suspicion until they checked up on me, or waited to see if I would give myself away. Apparently, I passed the test for I was taken from this home and was again on a bike.

The guide gave me a card with writing on it.

"The card says you are a worker in the district of Dinxperlo. Do not speak. If we are stopped and you see me take my card from my pocket, you do the same, but you must not speak!"

It was dark when I arrived at Somsenhuis. I was ushered into this large cozy room where I met you chaps.

· · · · ·

Chapter 11

Chuck Arrives

And so another night was over, and we went off to bed. The next day Frank returned from his jaunt with Co Hettinga. A couple of nights later, we were all standing out in the backyard watching the bomber stream of Lancasters returning from their target. We noticed a German night fighter firing at a Lancaster, which immediately burst into flames. We saw parachutes coming out of the bomber. We could easily see the parachutes because of the backdrop of the airplane on fire. It went into a slow spiral towards the earth and crashed about a mile away from us. As it went out of sight, we kept counting billowing parachutes.

"There should be one more," someone said. We never knew, then, if he got out.

Black Jan grabbed some of the boys and went off to try to pick up these fellows. The pilot had stayed with the airplane until his crew bailed out and then when he, himself, went out he was still wearing his goggles and helmet.

They did not find him that night, but next morning a man whose name was Mr. Harmsen brought the pilot to the farm. He had already been treated for his burns with goose grease. His face was burned all around the outside of where his goggles and helmet had been, especially on the right side. When they brought him up to our hiding place, all we had was a candle for light. They added more goose grease and the right side of his face seemed to look like a lump. It was awful.

"My God!" whispered Bob, "He must be in terrible pain!" It looked as though all the skin was almost completely burned off his face.

"His papers say his name is Charles Huntley, a Canadian." said Mr. Harmsen. "He was the pilot of that Lancaster."

We gave him as much room as we could so that he could be as comfortable as possible. The next day, the Underground brought him a doctor who sprinkled some kind of powder on his burns.

Chuck Arrives

The next day Frank returned and later Jan came and told us all the guns and ammunition had to be moved since the Germans were getting dangerously close. We did not feel that Chuck should be left alone so we drew straws, and I was the one chosen to stay with Chuck. That night, I helped load the cart and when we figured we had loaded everything, the five airmen; Frank, Joe, Bob, Jim, and Ted, took off walking down the road to 'de Bark'.

Chuck could not eat. In the healing process, he developed a huge ugly scab which encompassed part of his mouth and he could not open his mouth except for the use of a straw. He had to take his nourishment through a straw for many days. Chuck did not have enough space to rest and heal properly so the five airmen said they would remain at 'de Bark', where thirty or forty members of the Resistance were staying.

About this time, Hendrick, or Henk as we called him, the oldest Prinzen son, decided there were too many people at the farm. Part of the requirement by the Germans was to go and do certain work. So he chose to work at a German farm across the border.

Scabs were crusting around the edges of Chuck's wounds. In other words, he was beginning to heal, and most of the pain was gone by the time an Underground member came and told us to gather any ammo that had been missed, and go immediately to 'de Bark'.

Chapter 12

Danger!

When Chuck and I arrived, our fellow escapees were tense, sometimes talkative, sometimes silent, and they all had a look about them as though they had witnessed something terrible and wished they had not.

While Chuck and I helped the Underground load all the guns and ammunition in a cart, piece by piece I got the following story from them:

When they reached 'de Bark' after leaving the Prinzen farm, they settled in with some thirty or forty other Resistance workers and were soon caught up in the routine of the place. They stood guard duty, cleaned guns, practiced loading and unloading and sometimes a handful would go out at night on a sabotage assignment. Since this farmhouse was very much like Somsenhuis, there was a hayloft and that is where they all slept.

During the two days they were there, they went out on training exercise. One of these men who was carrying a Sten gun came back at night and as he got himself through a fence, he fired a single shot accidentally wounding himself in the back. He had to be carried back to the barn and was tended to there.

There were always guards around the outside of the building, 'Cockatoos' as Jim called them, and the following day, one came inside to warn everyone that there were two German soldiers approaching the building. A ranking Resistance worker shoved a Sten gun into Jim's hands and told him to keep an eye on the two women in the building. These two women were brought there because they had been fraternizing with Germans, and the Underground decided they could be more useful cooking for the Resistance workers. Anyway, they could not be completely trusted.

There was deathly silence in the farmhouse. Jim was holding the Sten gun at the head of one of the women and indicated in sign language that

119

she must be quiet or he would blow her head off. Whether he would have or not is another question.

We could hear the sounds of the two German soldiers breaking in or entering the rear of the farmhouse. Everyone sat silent, many holding their breaths when suddenly we heard the usual guttural tones of the German tongue in what appeared to be exclamations of surprise. They must have made their way into the area where the guns were stored — Sten guns, bazookas and ammunition.

The two Germans came in as though they thought the building was empty. They were completely taken by surprise to see several guns pointed at them, and so many people. They realized their mistake too late, and fought to get back out of the building. There was a scuffle and the soldiers got away and were heading across the open field on a run.

Long Henk, who after his previous night on exercises was sleeping in the hay, was roused by the sounds of the scuffle between the Germans and the Resistance men. Henk immediately went into action. He climbed down into the barn area. He grabbed the Sten gun and raced out the back door of the building and went after the two soldiers who were making a hasty retreat across the fields.

Henk apprehended the two soldiers and ordered them back to the farmhouse. When they were brought in, they were separated into two different rooms. One was a Major and the other was a sergeant.

A conference of the Underground people was called. Long Henk sent someone off to another farm in the area to get Black Jan. Some time later they both returned to the Underground hideout. Black Jan was wearing German jack-boots, a dark leather jacket and a black leather cap on his head. There was an ominous bulge underneath the leather jacket which turned out to be a Colt .45.

The five airmen could not understand most of the conversation that was going on between Black Jan, Long Henk and the Underground members, but it was obvious that they intended to interrogate the two prisoners. The Major was taken into the kitchen. He stood in front of a table. Black Jan sat behind the table.

"Would you like to see how we interrogate Germans?" he asked the airmen, and then invited them to have a seat and watch. They did. All the

German officer's papers and belongings from his pockets were laid out in front of him on the table. There were the usual things that soldiers keep in their pockets — photo of his wife and family, train and bus tickets. He was a fine-looking man, tall and fair-haired. He gave the impression of a very disciplined, well trained soldier.

Black Jan was questioning him in German, and we got the feeling he was not getting satisfactory answers. Black Jan was getting hostile and dressed the Major down by telling him what he thought of the Germans in no uncertain terms, that he was disgusted with Hitler and all he represented. He certainly left no stone unturned to let that man know he intended getting information from him. He pulled the .45 from under his jacket and held it against the German's head and we assumed he threatened to shoot the Major unless he divulged what they were doing in the area. We subsequently gathered from Black Jan later that the Major indicated to them that they had been sent out to inspect the area with regard to defensive positions they were anticipating they would need because the war was turning against them and they were retreating. He also divulged the fact that he had a driver and an aide in a staff car in the area and they were up the road some distance waiting to take them back to their headquarters.

The German officer was taken back to the middle of the barn where he was ordered to stand and the Sten gun was put into Jim's hands. Jim sat down on a box about eight or nine feet away from him. He cocked the gun and pointed it at his heart. The German was told in German not to move or he'd be killed.

They also interviewed the other soldier and when they ascertained that there was a staff car along the road, Long Henk put on the German officer's great coat, or maybe he borrowed one from one of the two German army deserters there. He and another member of the Underground left the farmhouse, and later returned with the driver of the staff car and the aide.

There was some discussion among the Allied airmen as to what the next move was likely to be. The Allied airmen agreed that the Germans had to be dispensed with and that they should be shot and the bodies buried under a haystack or something in the area. The Underground people,

121

however, were in authority there, and they decided that these four men should be hanged. They could take no chances, you see, not only for their own safety, but the safety of their families, and that included the Prinzen family we had sworn to protect.

It was an eerie scene. None of the Allied airmen took any part in the hanging. It was not done as skillfully as it might have been, perhaps, but those five airmen believed those men were throttled to death. The only active part any of the Allied men took in this deed was that Jim carried the body of the Major to the motor vehicle in which he arrived. A Resistance member helped him carry the body on a ladder. It was some distance down the road where the vehicle was parked.

Some of the airmen helped Underground members carry the other bodies to their motor vehicle where the Major's body was placed. Long Henk then drove it some distance away, but not before plastic explosives were set in the vehicle. They blew up the vehicle and all the bodies in it. They then returned to the barn.

"We tried to talk them out of hanging them," Bob said soberly, "And afterwards, we tried to convince them that burying them was a better idea, but the Underground leaders were adamant and so we could do nothing to stop them."

It was at that point that Chuck and I were sent for, with orders to go immediately to 'de Bark'.

As the group left with carts full of guns and ammunition, bazookas, and everything, we were all pretty quiet. Only the sound of soft footsteps and muffled rubber cart wheels could be heard. We cut across fields for about three quarters of a mile to a grain storage shed. It had a raised ramp on the front end for access for trucks that were storing the grain. There was access down under the flooring of this building through a trap door. There was only about two feet six inches of head room under that floor and the Allied airmen and another twenty or thirty Underground members went under the floor where all were instructed to lie quietly and we would have to lay up there until it was safe to go back to our respective farmhouses. It was icy cold, but there was straw to lie on.

There were a number of German soldiers out on a training exercise march — it seemed like a whole platoon. To make things more tense than they were already, the officer in charge of this group decided to halt everybody and have a smoke right outside this granary for a few minutes. We were all very relieved when they were called to attention and moved off.

While we were under that grain storage shed, I must have irritated a Dutchman in some way. Either by moving my feet, making a little noise, or because I was just a big man taking up too much room. At any rate, he pulled a gun on me. It really scared me. Someone told him to knock it off and the incident was over, but it indicated how tense we were.

After two nights of confinement in that crowded, freezing cold area, we were allowed to return to our respective places. The seven of us returned to Somsenhuis. We never again returned to 'de Bark'.

When we got back to the farmhouse, we were all pretty keyed up. A few days later, a German officer stopped by the farm and informed the Prinzen family that they were going to billet soldiers in and around their farm in two or three days.

That night, the seven of us gathered with the family to make plans. We did not have any place to go to keep away from the Germans so Papa Prinzen decided we should stay where we were and hide ourselves. We would rework the boards comprising the ceiling of the pump room which were also the boards that was the floor of our hiding place. When we got the details worked out, some of the men wanted to talk about what happened at 'de Bark'.

"You know what I can never forget? When they were questioning those Germans," Bob said, "It surprised me how brutal Black Jan was to them."

"Yes," Ted agreed, "He threatened them — he questioned them individually — interviewed them."

"It bothered me how forceful he was because I thought he was almost brutal," agreed Bob.

"You must remember what Jan has been through," Frank reminded them. "He was arrested four times by the Gestapo. Two of those times, if he had not escaped, he would have been shot. He has seen many of his friends arrested and then shot. Actually, what choice did he have but to eliminate them? Surely, he had to get what information he could from them first."

"It seems to me that the bodies should have been buried, though," put in Joe. "No bodies, no evidence."

"In retrospect," Frank said, "We know that to be true, but actually there was a time factor. It would have taken too much time to dig graves and bury the bodies. They probably just felt that at this stage of the war, there would not be a forensic testing. In view of how thorough the Germans are reputed to be, that should not have been part of the decision. You know, in our young lives as airmen up there in the sky, it is very probable that none of us have seen a dead enemy. I know I haven't. So it is bound to be a great shock to all of us."

Chapter 13

Chuck's Story

Since we had to rise early to get the hidden trap door completed on time, it was time to hit the hay. When we were all settled, I asked the big Canadian if he had healed enough to tell us his story. He said he would try. He related the following account to us:

• • •

On the night of February 21st, my crew was on our second mission. The same mission we went on the night before, over Roleinhurst. Because serial markings were used, the master bomber directed us to bomb the colored markers as indicated with the distance and time.

Everything was good and we turned to go back to base. As we were approaching the front lines, we could see it in the distance. The clouds had cleared out. Turning around at 6,000 feet and then descending to about 4,000 feet, we crossed the front lines.

According to regulations, we made periodic checks on the intercom on each crew member. The first indication I had that there was a problem was when I saw the starboard engine on fire. Apparently, no one had spotted an aircraft about when it attacked us. It was a night fighter and there were no symptoms of flak at the time.

The fire was intensifying in the wing. The main fuel line on the Lancaster runs along the leading edge of the main wing. Apparently, whatever shell had struck ruptured the main fuel line, and it was rapidly disintegrating that portion of the wing.

I immediately ordered the crew to jump. Then I tried to get recognition of each crew member. When this was done, everyone that I was aware of had left the aircraft.

Chuck's Story

When I first saw the fire, it had not developed too much, but there was such a rapid build up. It wasn't like an incendiary fire that builds up and dies down, it just accumulated, and built up.

There was congestion in the way within my section of the aircraft so I decided to leave through the pilot's upper hatch, which is right above the pilot's seat. I released the escape hatch above me and immediately saw that flames engulfed that side of the aircraft and it was impossible for me to leave that way.

Only my head and shoulders were out at the time, so I returned back into the cockpit. I looked around to see if the navigator, the bomb-aimer, and engineer were there as I made my way into the nose. I found one member still in the aircraft who was reluctant to depart. I helped him make up his mind and followed him out of the hatch.

The parachute harness had shifted around on me, but I eventually found the 'D' ring, pulled it, and the parachute opened successfully and I landed in a field.

I started to run to the birch trees at the side of a field, then realized I was dragging my parachute. I released the parachute from the harness, gathered it up and proceeded to the edge of the field leaving the parachute in the shrubbery.

When I first reached land, I thought I heard noises, but it was a fast drop and my ears were plugged. I heard what I thought to be the wireless operator, Flight Sergeant Romboy. I shouted a couple of times but after I cleared my ears, I couldn't hear the sound any more. I do not know if someone was shouting — maybe a member of my crew — but I heard no more sounds.

Soon after I landed alongside a roadway, I realized that when I attempted to leave the airplane through the upper hatch, I received flash burns on my face and it was getting exceedingly painful.

I knew I was very near the Dutch border so I began walking. I came to a farmhouse. There were three or four people watching the evening's proceedings and I walked up to them and said, "I am a Canadian." They did not recognize 'Canadian'. Then a woman said, "British Tommy?" I said "Yes". That was good.

She took me in the house and I was asked if I had any identification. I showed them my 'I' card [identity card]. The lady of the house saw I was in pain and applied some goose grease to the burns. The head of the household was concerned that I was who I said I was. I gave him every identification I had. I showed him my 'I' card and escape package that contained a compass, map, Dutch money, and they still were not convinced.

They suggested I stay in the shed until contact could be made to someone who could help me. Mr. J. H. Harmsen came to see me, asked me some questions, and said he would take me where there were other Allied airmen and better access to a doctor.

He brought me here to Somsenhuis. The next day the doctor came to see me.

• • • • •

Chapter 14

The Silent Seven

Right after breakfast next morning, we began on the project of the hidden trap door. Our tools consisted of a chisel, a small saw, a hammer, pencil, two pieces of wood, and a few nails. First, we numbered each piece of tongue and grove flooring, so that they would be replaced in the same order as they were removed. This was most important so that there would be no conspicuous differences or markings showing from underneath. The pieces of the extra wood were nailed crossways to the flooring to make it a unit easy to remove and replace. This was essential for food to be handed to us and a sanitation bucket taken down and handed back as quickly as possible in case German soldiers walked in the pump room.

The pump room was about ten feet by ten feet and the ceiling was a little low. I believe it was about seven feet from floor to ceiling. This enabled a person on the outside to hand a tray up through the trap door, or a bucket when needed. Someone from the upper floor could easily reach down a little way to receive whatever was being smuggled to them. Moreover, the pump was so situated that when it was in operation, the handle of the pump barred the door to the pump room. It was necessary to lock the door in order not to injure the knuckles of the person doing the pumping. This was a lucky and handy situation many times.

There were some nails that indicated where the center of the ceiling joists were located so we followed those nail markings to cut the boards down the middle over the joists. This allowed the ends of the trap door to rest on half of each ceiling joist. We removed the part of the tongue on the adjacent board that was permanent and uncut. When the door was in place, there was nothing obvious showing from underneath. The entrance we formerly used by way of a ladder was latched on the inside and the ladder was moved to another place near the dell.

When this was all completed, there was a practice session with the Prinzen family. A tray that might contain food or other essentials was handed up through the trap door, the sanitary bucket was handed up and down a few times to make sure it could all be done noiselessly.

That night, we knew we were up there for an indefinite period of time and our confinement began. It was the middle of March, 1945. Later that night, a member of the Underground came to talk to us in the hayloft. He told us he wished to convey the very great danger we were in and how important it was to be absolutely quiet. He also told us the Germans had forensic testing done of the four Germans that were hanged and found that they were not blown up in a strafing action from an Allied plane, but that they were actually hanged first.

In retribution, the Germans went to the nearby village and took thirteen hostages for each hanged man — fifty-two hostages in all — out into a field and tied them together and shot them. The remaining villagers were told that if anyone tried to bury them, put flowers around them or on them, or in any other way recognize the dead such as memorial services or wreaths hung in their memory, more hostages would get the same treatment.

We were already very frightened, and now we were also horrified. The Resistance member stayed with us that night, leaving before first light in the morning. This same member told us that on New Year's Day, after we had had our celebration of the New Year, they heard on the BBC that the German Luftwaffe had made a gigantic raid on an important air field in Belgium, turning a great number of Allied airplanes into rubble.

Through a loose roof tile and some glass tile, we watched as twenty or thirty Germans marched down the road to the Prinzen house, trailing two vehicles in which the officers rode driven by their chauffeurs.

Before very long, we heard the barn doors open and the sound of the vehicles being driven into the dell — as close under us as they could possibly get. We soon found out that the officers and their chauffeurs slept in their vehicles so that we knew they could hear us if we made the least sound because every night after that, we could hear someone snoring.

We tried so hard to keep quiet during the next few days that we did not have time to think how tedious it was to be in such a predicament.

However, Bob's cold which he had caught a couple of weeks previously, was now at the coughing stage. We had to sleep in shifts so there would be someone to put pillows and blankets over his head when he gave any indication of coughing. He got some sleep, but the persons on guard duty did not. Because of this problem, some of us slept in short naps during the day.

We could hear sounds of activities going on down below. One time, we could tell that one of the Germans was trying to make it with Truida who was objecting loudly. Papa Prinzen was there in no time at all, as he usually was when he was badly needed. His anger stopped the soldier from any ideas of a sexual nature he might have had. Papa's anger was more effective than a cold shower. The Major did not, apparently, interfere.

I was so nervous about noise that I put a piece of straw between the set of my ring and the Spartan head it contained. It seemed to me to be a little loose and I imagined I could hear it rattle every time I moved my hand.

Some of our time was filled with solitaire games, 'Guess which hand it's in', and anything we could dream up that was quiet. When we deduced that the troops were eating, we managed a few sit-ups and push-ups, quietly done of course, but we definitely did not get enough exercise. There were long periods of time when a man would seem to be day dreaming. Each was probably thinking about home, or a vacation they would like to take, or had taken, or a girl somewhere. I wondered if my wife and child had given me up for dead since I knew they had no way knowing otherwise.

One day, we heard a soft rapping on the trap door. Papa was there and told us that that group pulled out and another was coming in. We had about two hours to come down and get some exercise. We did so with enthusiasm. Each of us took a bath in the dell.

Our respite from confinement seemed all too short. We barely had enough time to get back in our hiding place. Even then, Derk locked the back door to slow them down and they had to go around to another door. One German in charge of the vehicles began cuffing Derk around for locking the door. As usual, Papa Prinzen stepped in and shouted at the soldier who backed off and apologized. Once again it was demonstrated to us that you must be harsh with the German soldiers or they will not respect you.

We still had the worry of Bob having a persistent cough, so we had to continue the system of the other six of us taking turns staying awake through the night to muffle Bob's cough whenever necessary.

The sleeping area was so small, when we lay down to sleep we had to sleep like spoons put together in a drawer. When one wanted to turn over, we all had to turn. There was no other way. There was still the ammunition at one end of the room taking up a great deal of space.

There was one distinct advantage about the room to which we were confined. There was a brick wall at one end. On the other side of this brick wall was a chimney from the kitchen stove. This didn't take up the whole expanse of the wall, however, because we could hear many activities going on in the residential part of the house especially in the kitchen where most of the living took place. So we were well aware that we could easily be heard as well. But at least the warm brick partially kept out the freezing cold that would otherwise have been still another situation contributing to our discomfort.

One day, I was down on my right side facing the wall, a patchwork quilt bunched under my cheek. Behind me, I could hear the careful, quiet breathing of the six other men in the tiny space. We were so crowded, we could almost hear the burbles and rumblings of each others' bodies.

As often happened, the door opened in the pump room below. We could clearly hear men's voices, and the sound of water being pumped into a basin. One of the Germans was washing up, or perhaps preparing to shave. Papa's familiar voice could be heard softly now and then, addressing the German as 'Major'. Papa was answered only by an occasional grunt and a splash of water.

We were very still, scarcely breathing, when Bobby moved his injured leg just a little for better comfort. His flight boot made a scraping sound on the wooden floor of the loft where there was a thin spot in the straw covering. We all tensed, rigid with fright. I concentrated hard on the pattern in the rough wood wall so that the panic welling up in my stomach could not force any sound from between my lips.

"*Vas is Das?*" the Major asked.

"Just one of our cats chasing a mouse!" Papa quickly replied in Dutch. The officer grunted once and the door closed as both men returned to the kitchen.

"That was bloody close!" Frank ventured a cautious whisper. We all sighed with relief.

Jim, lying in the middle, carefully began to turn. As though someone had blown a silent signal, the rest of us began to turn over to lie for awhile on our left sides. Each man's right leg was little numb. The quilt over the layer of straw was not thick enough to soften the hard wooden floor. The evenings for the German soldiers were understandably better than ours. However, there were times when we enjoyed their evenings, too, to a certain extent. While in the parlor around the organ, they would sing songs that we could easily hear. A lot of these melodies were familiar. You could even say that we considered them our own melodies. We heard the 'Beer Barrel Polka' — in German of course — and hymns that were familiar to us. One German played an accordion and another played a trumpet and there was an officer in a completely different room playing the harmonium (reed organ) so there was sometimes a concert, of sorts, to enjoy. The Prinzen family joined in with this singing and friendliness, which they later told us they did to throw off any chance of suspicion. Furthermore, they felt that if it was discovered that they were helping Allied airmen, maybe the Germans would be more lenient with them than otherwise. Of course, we all realized later on that it wouldn't have made any difference.

One of the things that happened was that Jan Ket would nip in and out about four in the morning. How, we never knew. There were guards all around the place. He would come dressed in black puttees — the balloon type — like a motorcycle rider. He wore an A-2 jacket, shoulder holster and yachting cap — all black — and he wandered in and out among those Germans as if he were one of them, and he was never stopped or questioned.

Several times a German soldier or officer would get angry when one of them wanted to go into the pump room to shave or wash and the door would be locked. When Papa was asked by a German why the door was locked, he would answer, "To keep some damn fool from opening the door while the pumping is going on and injuring the person doing the pumping." Suggestions were made to Papa how that problem could be eliminated. We looked at each other each time wondering what would happen next. Papa just listened and said *"Ja, Ja,"* but did nothing about it.

Actually, most of the time Papa Prinzen and one of the boys were involved in taking care of our needs, handing us food, passing the toilet bucket up or down, supplying us with water or coffee. The pump room door was locked, Papa and one of the boys locked inside. Papa would hand us up what we needed, while one of the boys would pump water or rattle milk cans together.

I was pretty tense most of the time causing fast heart beats sometimes or a tightness in the stomach. I felt great stress a lot and I am sure I was not alone. One time, Ted got a little noisy, I thought, and I hissed at him to knock it off. He whispered right back, "Gee, do I have to be absolutely quiet all the time?" And, of course, he did and we all did, but because we were so tense, I probably only imagined that he was getting noisy.

Their officers kept the cars in the barn. The chauffeurs stayed with the cars, night and day. One car was almost right underneath us with only an inch flooring separating us. He was near enough for us to hear him cough now and then as he moved about the car.

When Moeder cooked, no one seemed to notice that she cooked twice as much food as was necessary and when she made coffee, she made two pots of coffee, one for the soldiers billeted in the house, and the other was smuggled to us in our hiding place.

One day, Truida had just handed us a plate of sandwiches and we closed the trap door. Before she got her arms lowered — that very second — a German walked in. She had forgotten to lock the pump room door.

"What are you doing?" he asked.

"Just stretching," she answered. "There is so much work to do. I get tired sometimes."

Above her head, we were all frozen in place. When the door closed, we were able to relax and enjoy the sandwiches.

One night when the Germans were entertaining themselves in the house by playing the harmonium and singing, they sang the song called 'Madeleine' and we sat around in a circle as Frank whispered a partial translation:

When we were in the service,
near our barracks there was a small café.
The proprietor had an attractive daughter,
named Madeleine.
  Chorus
One day having marched past the café,
and given Madeleine our EYES RIGHT.
The Lieutenant said, "If you give an EYES RIGHT
without my word of command,
You will all be locked up in the guardhouse".

There was a lot more to it than that, of course, and we got to know it pretty well. We even sang it softly a few times — barely above a whisper — when the Germans were especially enthusiastic about it and were singing loudly.

Meanwhile, the front lines were moving toward us and the sound of guns got louder each day. It did not relax us. It only caused more fright and tenseness.

The casual attitude adopted by the Dutch toward the soldiers impressed us. Once we heard Truida ask the Germans if they had ever captured any American or British pilots. The soldiers replied that they had not.

"The reason you cannot," she taunted, "is because the Dutch have a system to pick them up and hide them on the farms. I have heard of one farm that has seven pilots in hiding."

I am not the only one who was holding his breath. We waited and we waited, but the challenge was not taken up by the Germans.

One day towards the end of our stay, one of the soldiers was holding little Benny on his lap. Benny must have said something because the soldier asked, "Where did you get that idea?"

"From Frank." said Benny.

"Who is Frank?" the soldier asked.

Benny had gotten accustomed to calling Frank Dell 'Frank' and the Germans would not pronounce it that way.

"Oh, that's someone he knew once," replied one of the Prinzens, and the soldier was satisfied.

As the front kept moving closer, there was fighter activity overhead. We watched through our peeking places in the roof. On one occasion there was quite a lot of activity over an area not far away, and of course the German anti-aircraft guns nearby popped away at them. This one time the German soldiers came running back into the farmhouse to get their guns. Farmer Prinzen asked them what they were going to do with the guns. They replied that if the aircraft guns knocked any of them down and any of the flyers parachuted, they were going to shoot them as they came down. Fortunately, none of them had to jump.

During our confinement in the straw, I came down with scabies. Twice, the Prinzen women took our underclothing and washed and boiled them, and the Underground took our outer clothing one time to 'de Bark' and cleaned them with gasoline. Still, the scabies persisted. I was sure I would go mad, but I had no choice but to bear it the best I could. I said nothing much about it to the others and very possibly they had the same problem, but I'll never know.

The front moved closer and closer. Came the time when we were literally in No-Man's-Land. The Allies were shooting from one side and the Germans from the other. Many of these bullets and explosions were right over the farmhouse. The Germans had their 88mm guns with a flat trajectory and the shells would come zooming just over our roof, and the British shells, fired from 25-pounder howitzer high angle guns, would go rather higher up and would make a characteristic noise as they went that way. We knew the Prinzen family had moved down to the basement as no food or anything else had passed through the trap door for several hours.

We could not get out. Not only were we trapped between two warring factions, we were trapped in an attic which was our prison, and could be our fiery coffin. We did not know where the Germans were who were billeted in the farmhouse. We assumed some of them were in the basement with the Prinzen family. Their basement was very small and could only hold a limited number of bodies no matter how much they squeezed together. We had to figure that there were some Germans who were left in

The Silent Seven

the house where we would be seen if we tried to leave. At that point, nothing would please them more than to find seven Allied airmen hiding in the hayloft.

So we stayed. We watched the war going on over our heads. Most likely, some of us prayed. Others seemed fascinated by their own predicament.

A farmhouse nearby was hit and burst into flames. If the Prinzen farmhouse were hit, especially the hayloft where we were hiding, we knew we would have a quick and fiery death.

We were anxious and touchy. By mutual agreement, we talked very little, not only because we were scared, but because we were holding ourselves together and a word or two could trigger panic or cause someone to lose control. Night came and the pounding continued for a long time and then it gradually began fading away into the distance.

Chapter 15

March 30, 1945

At morning light, Papa rapped on the trap door. "They are all gone," he said. "You can come down now. The Tommies are coming."

And we did come down as fast as we could. We opened the side door that opened to the southeasterly direction and we watched the shells bursting on the road, so I think the Germans must have pulled out during the night. We had never seen shells bursting like that before, and they were hitting the ground with a great spurt of fire and would roar on the road as they exploded. One after the other, there were these great bursts of flame about a mile away.

Someone pointed out that there was a tank on fire out there, but we soon discovered that it was a tank with orange color on the top to alert our fighters and bombers that the tank and its occupants were Allies.

We started to hurry out to the tank until we realized we were not in our regular uniforms and were really not completely wearing regulation clothes at all.

About that time, the eldest son, Henk, returned home. He told us the Germans had all gone. He volunteered to go out to where the tank was and speak to the soldiers and tell them not to fire on us. We were aware of the danger of running towards them, especially Frank, who was wearing his RAF blues. He could have been mistaken for a German soldier. Henk came back to say they were Canadians and it was safe to go to them now because they were told that seven Allied airmen had been hiding out at this farm and that they wanted to let their families know they were OK. We ran out across the field to this small scout car and that was a wonderful sight to see. There was a typical Cockney driver in the front of this small car and he offered us cigarettes.

March 30, 1945

Bob smoked like a starving man and coughed afterward for two days. The officer in charge of this scout vehicle was preoccupied with his wireless equipment. He was surprised to see us.

"We are British and American pilots and we have been hiding up here in the hayloft."

"Jolly good show!" The officer replied and we all laughed. "I haven't seen anything like this since the days back in France when they had Allied airmen come out of hiding."

He turned to his radio equipment and called the officer in charge of the patrol and the officer told him he couldn't talk at the moment because he was having a bit of a tussle with a German tank. So we just stood by this vehicle for a few minutes, and then there was an answer back.

"What do you have to report," came over the wire. We could hear heavy gunfire coming through the wire as well. "Well done. Now that I've knocked him out of the way, let's hear about what's going on down there?"

Arrangements were made for an amphibian (an Alligator) to take us back to Somsenhuis where we said our emotional goodbyes to this brave and wonderful family and gathered together what belongings we had.

We were transported to a place about a mile down the road where we were debriefed for a short period. We could see some captured German soldiers being held there as we walked to this field station.

Black Jan was standing at the rear of the amphibian. He took great delight in calling out what were probably strong words to groups of German soldiers who had been captured and when we reached the army camp, Jan was so impressed. He had never seen such a might of armor, and there were hundreds and hundreds of armored vehicles, virtually bumper-to-bumper.

We were taken to the town of Tilburg in a canvas-covered caravan where there was a reception center. We were re-equipped with clothes, plain khaki battle dress and trousers, and a khaki beret. There was no rank or insignia on our clothes. These clothes were Canadian. We were a fairly motley crew. We were given a medical inspection and within twenty-four hours, we were driven to Brussels where I had my second soaking bath in two days as part of the treatment for the case of scabies I had developed. With this continuous treatment that included a certain medicinal salve, by the time I reached Paris, the blisters had pretty much dried up.

From Brussels, Frank, Chuck and Jim were flown back to England, while we four Americans were flown to Paris, where we were, at last, back in American Military hands. We were there about four days. We were then flown back to England in a C-47.

Chapter 16

Doris's Story

• • •

A few days after Thanksgiving in the fall of 1944, I was getting a little worried since no letter had arrived from Owen for some time. Owen wrote nearly every day. This was not like him. Something was wrong. That morning, I drove to the Southern Pacific Depot just across the river to see Owen's older brother, Thurman. Thurman was the station agent in Fair Oaks, California, at the time and he also received and distributed telegrams and I knew he would tell me the truth.

As I went through the door of the small station, I saw Thurman working on some papers and asked if I could disturb him for a moment. He stood up and greeted me in a friendly manner and indicated a chair. I sat down and got right to the point. I didn't have any time to spare. There was a baby at home and I wanted to get back to her as soon as I could. I folded my hands tightly in my lap and asked him a question.

"Because I am your sister-in-law and Owen is your brother, would you keep a telegram from me until after the Holidays so as not to spoil it for me?"

"Not on any day whatever it is. It is against the law," he answered. I burst into tears. My fears intensified, but I had my answer. Now all I had to do was wait. Wait for good news or bad news. Wait and worry.

I stood up and Thurman stood up too and put his arm around my shoulders in sympathy. Before returning home, I made my daily stop at the post office. No letter. I drove home feeling a little lost, as usual. What has happened to Owen? Can a person just disappear? I'd read enough stories, fictional and non-fictional, to know that people do disappear without a trace.

Doris's Story

I finally decided to try the Red Cross. I contacted the nearest Red Cross office. They took all the information that they needed from me and said they would notify me of their findings, if any. I went on with my daily routine of taking care of baby Candy, and helping my Mom. I lived with my parents while Owen was gone. That was where he left me and that is where he expected to find me if and when he returned home.

Candy was an easy baby to care for. She had her hours reversed, however. She wanted to sleep all day and stay awake all night. This was not only hard on me, but on my parents as well since her crying kept them both awake at night. I spent my days mostly caring for her, bathing her, and playing with her. My idea was that perhaps if I could keep her awake all day, she would sleep at night. It didn't always work, for a variety of reasons. She either got fussy because she was tired, or she slipped off to sleep when my back was turned.

My sisters, Nadine and Inez, and my sister-in-law, Alice, were also without husbands. The difference was they were hearing regularly from their husbands and I was not. They tried in many ways to cheer me up. They took me to movies, lunch, shopping, church, choir practice and a variety of things. Sometimes I did not go. Sometimes I did not want to go; I just wanted to wallow in my misery and hold my baby. I responded to their trying to cheer me the best I could.

About the middle of December, soon after the news informed us that a number of B-17's had been lost over Germany, Evelyn, Thurman's daughter and Owen's niece, brought me a Christmas gift she purchased for Owen at his instructions. It was a gaily-wrapped package.

I couldn't wait to open it, and everyone urged me to do so figuring, I suppose, that I needed the boost in morale that it would undoubtedly give me. I opened it and found a lacy, luscious nightgown. I wept all over the top of the folded nightgown until Inez snatched it away and handed me a handkerchief.

Christmas came and went. It was during this period of time that I told Nadine, if Owen is dead, I will somehow build a house some place for Candy and me. I was so grateful I had Candy with me. She was a sweet baby and good company, in spite of her occasional crying. Sometimes I wondered if she sensed that her Daddy was missing. I couldn't get by without her, I was certain. I tried to be brave and strong for her, but sometimes, after she had gone off to sleep, I wept quietly for a long time until I finally fell into an exhausted sleep.

New Year's came and went. It had been so long. The Red Cross notified me that they had found no trace of my husband, but the Red Cross worker I talked with very kindly added that that only meant he was not a prisoner of war. He could be hiding out somewhere. I hadn't thought of that. So I got out my map of Europe. I followed the war news of Europe as closely as possible and made marks where there were reported activities of B-17's. I didn't know until much later that I had him pretty well pinpointed. I marked Misburg as I did all the other targets named in the news, but I didn't know that was the mission where Owen's plane was hit.

As always I tried, after each report, to imagine the pilot and crew trying to get back to England. If their plane was hit, about what route would be taken to limp back to England?

Of course, I kept this up way past the time Owen's airplane went down because I didn't know.

I received a letter from one of the mothers of a young man from Owen's plane. He was her son and a prisoner of war. She copied her letter word for word. "We are all safe." So, whether he meant Owen or whoever was on the same mission, there was no clue there either.

The next day, I left Candy with Mom and went with Nadine and baby David. She needed to go shopping. Afterward, I took Candy over to my brother-in-law's house to read the letter to him and his wife.

I tried to get active in local affairs. Inez and I went to a community meeting. Its primary purpose was to organize those willing to work for the betterment of our town. I, rather reluctantly, ran for secretary since that was the skill I could do best. I did not win, but was offered the job of assistant secretary. It seemed, however, that the lady who became secretary did not like me. I wasn't very lovable. I was worried all the time and was, unfortunately, sometimes short with my answers. I seemed to hear other voices and kept listening to those far away voices. One sound stood out — the voice of my husband. Thinking about him and wondering where he

Doris's Story

was or if he still lived occupied all my waking hours and a lot of my sleeping hours as well. It was very hard for me to be in a crowd. So I did not accept the job of assistant secretary. It might have been good for me, but I doubt if it would have been good for the town.

In February, 1945, we heard from my brother, Glen. He wanted to make a special trip home and didn't have the money to pay for his trip. I never understood why the CeeBees did not back him in this, but we could not have Alice hoping he could get home when he couldn't, so I dug up the money to bring him home.

The end of February brought the beginning of spring. Never before did I need the boost that yellow daffodils, tulips, almond blossoms, and acacia could give me. The major part of winter was over, although we would certainly have more rain and cold. The sight of those beautiful blossoms filled my heart and sight and nose with wonderful smells and promises. I began to lift my head sometimes and look up at the sky. I would talk to Owen as if he were there somewhere in the clouds. 'Owen,' I whispered 'where are you? Are you still alive? Are you hurt? Is someone looking after you?'

I am not psychic, I'm pretty sure, but I kept on hearing Owen's voice in my head.

In the middle of March, I still hadn't received any word. I had long ago stopped going down to the post office. It was too painful. I would run into elderly friends from the church. With tear-filled eyes, they always asked about Owen, and I got to where I could not answer them anymore. When I told the postmistress, Mrs. Webb, about it she told me, "Doris, you stay home. I'm not supposed to, but I will call you. You just stay home with your baby until you hear from me." And so, from then on, I stayed at home and waited.

By this time, I was depressed and felt very old. I was under a lot of stress. I was always catching a cold. First, Candy would have it, then I would have it, having caught it from her, and so it went.

Nadine and I went to a movie, 'To Have and Have Not' with Marlene Dietrich and Humphrey Bogart. That afternoon, we heard rumors that the war was over, but soon after it was denied.

My sisters took me shopping and I ended up buying a flame-colored dress and a grey dress. I suppose I did this to have either outcome covered. I bought the dresses at the Village Vanity for $20.00.

After April 1st, I planned to go with Inez to Los Angeles since she hoped to meet her husband, Bill, who was due in port very soon, but she got word at the last minute that he would not be in for another month.

April 13th, the telephone rang. It was Mrs. Webb telling me there was a letter waiting for me from Owen. It was mailed from Paris. He wrote this letter with the assurance that I had already heard that he was all right. The Canadian Tank Corps, who liberated the seven fliers, said that they would notify each man's family. They did not. Anyway, assuming I had heard he was OK, he wrote, 'I am in Paris. I've been in the Follies. Having a wonderful time! Be home as soon as I can get transportation.'

After May 1st, I got another letter. Owen was still in England. He said he would be home soon, but was having trouble trying to get transportation. There were a lot of men and women to haul back over the Atlantic. He wrote that he would be going to Santa Monica for rehabilitation and that wives were welcome, too, and at a very reduced cost.

On the 13th of May, Owen sent me eighteen red roses for Mother's Day. At the end of May a beautiful hunk of man arrived home with perfume from Paris, and a lot of hugs.

A few days later, he left for Santa Monica by Air Force facilities and I drove the car down for a wonderful vacation at a beautiful, elegant hotel overlooking the beach. The war officially ended while we were there, and we celebrated.

Everybody went wild, including us!

• • • • •

Epilogue
Doris Mayberry, 1995

As of this writing, Frank Dell and his wife Isabel live part of the year in England and part in Australia. Frank became a pilot for British Overseas Airways and was promoted to the rank of Captain, and continued to fly until his age required he work at a desk. His wife has spent some time, off and on, as a model for the mature figure. Frank has been very active in the Escapee Society from its inception, filling various offices. He and Isabel travel to Underground reunions in Europe, Canada, and the United States. Frank and Isabel had three boys; one lives in England, one in Australia, and one in California*.

Joe Davis continued his career in the military. He had additional assignments, one of which allowed him to visit the Prinzen family before they immigrated to Canada. He was awaiting an assignment while with his wife and family in Colorado when he took ill. After considerable tests of various sorts, he was diagnosed as having a brain tumor. He died of this affliction in the mid-1960's.

After coming home, Bob Brown married a girl he had known before he left for Europe. Her name is Martha. They adopted two children, a boy and a girl. For a few years, Bob was an independent plumber, then later accepted a position with a plumbing contractor in San Francisco.

---

* In 2014, Frank Dell published his own wartime account in the book, *Mosquito Down: The Extraordinary Memoir of a Second World War Bomber Command Pilot on the Run in Germany and Holland*, with Brett Piper.

Owen went back to government work and retired after thirty-one years. He felt he was too young to retire, so he played with a few jobs and landed a position with Aerojet. At the age of sixty-five, he retired for good. He never forgot his experiences at Somsenhuis and kept in touch with the Prinzen family as well as possible; telephoning Dora (Moeder) every year on her birthday in January. He and his wife, Doris, had three children, two boys and a girl. The girl, Candace Joan, was born before he left for overseas.

Ted Roblee returned to Milwaukee only to find that his father had moved. Since he did not know where, he inquired of some friends who gave him the new address. He went to the house which was answered by a woman he did not know. "I am your new step-mother, please come in."

Ted went to college under the GI Bill and, after completing his education, obtained a position with a large farm equipment firm and for several years was in charge of sales for the Latin American branch of that company.*

Jim Strickland returned to Australia, married and they produced three boys. Jim worked for many years in real estate and did quite well. They now live in a very nice retirement home in Australia.

Chuck Huntley healed very well. For awhile, all that could be seen of a burn on his right cheek was that slight pinkish look that was mentioned before. However, even that disappeared shortly. He continued in his military career and then he and his wife bought a bar and hotel located in the southeastern part of British Columbia, Canada. When they decided to retire, they sold the business and lived for a few years in Dodsland, Saskatchewan, to care for Chuck's elderly father. When his father died, they moved back to British Columbia to a mobile home park. They produced a happy family.

---

* In 2013, six months after his death, Ted Roblee's daughter, Mary Ellen Simms, published her father's previously-written account of his wartime experience in the book, *World War 2 Memories: Behind the German Enemy Lines*.

Epilogue

In 1946, all members of the Prinzen family, except Truida, immigrated to Canada after their beloved Somsenhuis had burned to the ground during a violent lightning storm the previous year. They started life in their new country and all did quite well.

Papa contracted cancer, probably from the tension during the war, and in the early 1960's, he died in Canada. Moeder and her other nine children carried on without him. All married and had families. Marinus died from injuries incurred during a farm machinery accident.

Moeder lived to age 93. She suffered from diabetes and as a consequence had to have part of one leg removed. She spent the rest of her life in a rest home after that. This was for about two years. She died in the fall of 1994. Other than her eight surviving children, she had over fifty grandchildren and several great-grandchildren. Frank Dell was with her a few days before her death.

Truida and her family continue to live in Holland. They built a new house on the site where Somsenhuis stood.

Jan Ket died of cancer and Emmy is residing in Den Dolder. Henk van t'Lam also died of cancer and his widow lives in Overveen. Henk ten Have has retired from farming. He turned his farm over to his son and their family. Henk lives near Wesepe. Co Hettinga lives in Gaanderen. Herman Overmars, in the area of Olst, died, and Toni, his widow, continues to live in the old home. All live in The Netherlands. Sam Stirum (Count) and his wife, Francoise, live in Switzerland.

The rest of Owen's crew came back from the war alive. They had been taken prisoners and had had a bad time for awhile, but they got home. Their B-17 had crashed on a farm field near an abbey. A farmer was in the field at the time and was killed by the crash. The monks from the abbey rushed to the site to be of help, if possible. They discovered the airplane was without a crew, and that the farmer was dead. They transported the farmer to his home where they were asked to give him the last rites, and arranged for his burial. The monks later returned to the airplane and salvaged what they could. The oxygen tanks were made into buckets and any item that could be used was brought back to the abbey.

I apologize for leaving anyone out of this list. So many years have elapsed, it is difficult to mention everyone's name.

Owen and Bob did not keep in touch very well for several years until one day Owen had a feeling he wanted to see and talk to Bob. He wrote to Frank who had been corresponding with Bob through the years, received his address and wrote a letter to Bob. Bob answered with one letter and the next letter was written by Martha. The following letters explain, in part, how and why this book was written:

February 2, 1963

Dear Frank,

I hope you and your wife and the boys are well and had a happy Christmas Holiday. I imagine that hints of spring will soon be in the air in England, and that it will be a beautiful one.

You probably find it peculiar to hear from me at this time since we have only corresponded during the holiday season. Perhaps I'm getting old. I am getting sentimental.

After 18 years I am thinking more and more of our experiences during the war. I wonder about Bob. I know he lives somewhere in California, probably not far from my house. It's ridiculous that I do not have his address, but I don't. I have a feeling you have been writing to him now and then, so would know where he lives.

Could you write me his address as soon as is convenient? I feel a very strong urge to get in touch with him.

Warm and friendly greetings to you and your family.

Owen.

Epilogue

March 1, 1963

Dear Owen,

To say that I was surprised to receive your letter at such an unusual time of the year would be putting it mildly. We are all well here — a sniffle now and again, but nothing serious.

We have had no hint of spring, as yet, for at this very moment it is quite dark outside and raining hard. I should imagine, however, that some of your days in California are very beautiful now. It must be very much like Spain, and that is where all of us are off to tomorrow morning. I wanted to answer your letter right away lest I forget in the excitement.

I must apologize for having taken so long to answer you, but the hours I have been putting in of late at the airline company have been long. There was a reorganization in process, and I was closely involved.

Bob's address:(deleted)

It was grand hearing from you and we look forward to your next letter, telling us of your contact with Bob and Martha. Give a special 'hello' to them from us. They have adopted two children, a girl and a boy.

Warmest greetings to Doris and the two boys and Candace Joan.

Frank.

March 10, 1963

Dear Bob,

Surprise! I'll bet you never expected to hear from me again. The years have slipped by so rapidly, but I've thought of you many times. I just never seemed to have the time to try to get in touch with you.

However, lately I've been thinking of you more and more and of the winter we all spent at the farm during the war. I wrote to Frank to get your address because I knew he would have it. I just received his answer a few days ago.

To tell you a little about myself, as you know we have a daughter, Candy, born before I went to England. Remember, I was the only father hidden at the farm? And everyone called me 'Pop'. However, during the years, two boys, Bob and Dan, joined the family and Doris and I have had our hands full.

I work for the government and am still involved with airplanes, my first love. I don't fly them, I repair them. I don't want to fly a jet. I think they go too fast for me, or I go too slow for them. The job is OK as jobs go, and I have done better than most.

If you could tell me what day of the week we could find you and your family at home, we would like to stop by some time. We often drive to the bay area for pleasure, and would enjoy it even more by visiting you.

Frank tells me that you have a boy and a girl. Sounds like a wonderful family.

Frank and Isabel send their greetings. Let us hear from you soon. Say 'hello' to Martha and the children.

Owen.

March 17, 1963

Dear Owen,

It has been a few years hasn't it? I am like you. I have thought about you many times, but have not acted upon my thoughts. Like you, there has been so much effort making a living that there never seemed to be a chance to do much else.

Since we last had contact, I have made several changes. I sold my property in Lake County, and borrowed more money to go into business for myself, as a plumbing contractor.

I worked hard and paid back the money I borrowed, but was never able to get ahead after the debts were paid, so I closed the business and now work for a San Francisco contractor. I make more money than I made in my own business, but I miss the independence of working for myself.

Martha and I were married in 1947. We wanted children, but I could

Epilogue

not have them. After talking to the doctor, I learned why. You had not arrived at the farm yet when Frank, Jan and I went out on a supply drop. I was accidentally hurt. The pain was so bad I thought I was going to die, but it didn't hurt very long and there was little after-effect, so I virtually forgot about it.

Anyway, we adopted a boy and girl. The girl looks like my side of the family and the boy takes after some of Martha's family, so we are very fortunate.

You will find us at home nearly every weekend, and you are welcome any time. I have a cousin living near you and when we go to see her, we will also stop by and see you.

Let us hear from you soon.

Bob.

April 11, 1963

Dear Owen,

This is Bob's wife answering your letter of March 10th. I certainly wish this writing could be under much happier circumstances. Bob was taken to the hospital last Friday, underwent surgery on Tuesday. Owen, the children and I won't have Bob with us for long. When they operated they found he had extensive cancer, the liver is almost completely deteriorated and his intestines are very bad.

I know he would love to see you once again if you could possibly come down. He is here at St. Francis Memorial Hospital in San Francisco on Bush and Hyde Streets, Room 504a. The doctor says he might be coming home in about 10 days but who knows. The good Lord will have His way.

Owen, I've been married to the most wonderful guy a woman could possibly have lived with for the past fifteen years. Knowing what I know now, I would do just what I did all over again if I had the chance. He has given us the best years of his life.

Try to make it to the hospital. You come anytime. The visiting hours are 2 to 8, but they aren't particular.

I am sitting beside Bob in his room and he sends his best regards. He has had a shot to ease the pain, and he dozes frequently.

Hope to be seeing you soon.

Regards, Martha.

P.S. I also must get a letter off to Frank.

April 15, 1963 (Monday after Easter Sunday)

Dear Frank,

This is not an easy letter for me to write, and not an easy letter for you to receive. After getting Bobby's address from you, I immediately wrote a letter to him. I received a reply almost right away, and my wife and I planned when we could go there for a visit. Family problems came up and before we could make it, we received a letter from Bob's wife Martha.

She told us Bob was in the hospital and had been in surgery for cancer. It's terminal, Frank. He hasn't very much longer to live. Doctors say from two weeks to maybe a year. I wish there was some way he could see you again. He spoke of you and Jan several times. My being there started him reminiscing.

We visited him yesterday in the hospital. His attitude about life and death has not changed. He is facing his situation squarely as he did during the war. He talks of his own death calmly, his wife stays with him in his room. They spend a lot of time — when he's awake — just talking. When he sleeps, Martha prays. She sleeps very little.

I'm sorry to have to write you this sad news.

Greetings to your family.

Owen.

Epilogue

Same day

Dear Jan,

I have to relate bad news. This letter will be short and sad.

Bobby is very ill with cancer. Doctors give him two weeks to possibly one year. I have already written to Frank in England.

Doris and I have been to see him. He talked a lot of you and Frank and of the time we were all hiding at the Prinzen farm. Is there any way at all that you could come to California to see him? I know how hard it would be for me to travel that far because of the expense, but if you can find a way — any way at all — it would be a wonderful thing for Bob, and would fulfill a dying wish.

Sincerely, Owen.

[One year later.]

April, 1964

Dear Ted,

I was determined to contact you, and tried three cities in Wisconsin before you were located. I should have tried Waukesha first, but no matter. Thanks for giving me your address.

As I explained over the phone. Bobby died last week, and was buried at National Memorial [Golden Gate National Cemetery] in San Francisco with full military honors. As I promised, I am writing you the details of what has happened.

A year ago, after 18 years, I wrote and asked Frank for Bob's address. I found he lived only one and a half hours from me by car. Silly, isn't it, after all this time?

By the time I had contacted Bobby, he was in the hospital and had had an exploratory operation.

I wrote Frank who told his boss the story and Frank was given a free 'seat available' ticket from London to San Francisco via Toronto.

I wrote to Jan. I knew he would want to know, but I was uncertain of his ability to find a way to see Bobby.

One morning at work I was walking from one part of the shop to another when an assistant came out of the shop office and called to me. "Hey, Owen, the Pentagon's on the phone. Wants to speak to you!"

I just looked at him thinking 'what a clown'. I figured he meant my wife was calling me.

I said 'hello' and a man's voice said, "This is Colonel Hossidy (sp) of the Dutch Embassy. Is this Owen Mayberry?"

I sort of snapped to attention and said, "Yes, Sir!" and nearly dropped the phone.

"I have your letter to Jan Ket in front of me, and before I follow through with this, I want to know if Robert is still alive."

"Yes, Sir, last week he was, and I'd be informed if anything happened."

"Thank you very much. Goodbye," and he hung up the phone leaving me dazed, stupidly looking at the phone in my hand.

Next, a letter arrived from Jan saying he had tried to come to Bobby by military transport, but it could not be done. Then he wrote proudly that his country's Prince Bernhard, who is a member of the Board for KLM airlines, gave him a complimentary ticket to San Francisco after he heard the story from his military secretary.

As soon as technical details for overseas travel were taken care of, Jan packed his bags and sent me a telegram to meet him at the San Francisco International Airport.

Frank and Jan were not here at the same time, but I got all the conversations on tape.

The story will be complete soon and because you were at the farm also, I'll send you a taped copy of it. You'll be hearing from me later.

Owen.

Epilogue

Six years later: The 25th Anniversary of the liberation of Holland ...

On March 30, 1970, Owen and I left Los Angeles International on a chartered flight. Our destination was Holland for the 25th celebration of liberation and the Underground reunion. We landed in Frankfurt, Germany, and were met by Jan Ket and his son, Benny.

They drove us to their home in Den Dolder, Holland, where Emmy was waiting. We would be guests in their home they named 'De Bark' in remembrance of the barn where the Underground members were quartered and where a lot of activities occurred that are related in this book.

'De Bark' was beautiful and typical in our imagination as to what a Dutch home should be; from the lace curtains, which we found out were hand crocheted by Emmy, to the flower room, a sunny room that was glass-enclosed on the north side of the dining room. Emmy soon lost her fear of 'those rich Americans' and we became very good friends, especially when she found out we were not rich, but like so many other Americans.

After one day of rest, Jan began his self-appointed task of being our tour guide throughout much of Holland. We saw castles, reindeer, canals and dykes, the Zuider Zee, plus several beautiful old churches both inside and out. Very impressive sights were the memorials erected to remember the tragic days of German invasion and occupation.

At Amersfoort, there had been a concentration camp for Dutch people taken prisoner for such small infractions as listening to the BBC or a more serious offence such as sabotage and all those in between. Jan led us along a sandy path toward a cul-de-sac. At the end was a statue that depicts a Dutch man in traditional clothing. The left hand of the statue is pulling his jacket to one side baring his chest. The chest shows hunger. His right hand at his side forms into a fist. Around the base of the statue are four white doves. All around the banks that form the cul-de-sac, German soldiers with rifles used to stand guard to prevent any Dutchman from escaping before execution. Unlike the back yard of the Ket home where we stayed, we heard no birds singing in the trees at this sad place.

One year later...

    We watched the passing scene, Owen and I. The bucolic countryside just outside of Bloomfield, Ontario, Canada, was such a contrast to the Central Valley of California in July, which is our home. The beautiful, green landscape was capped with a clear blue sky.

    As we drove along, I day-dreamed of our trip we took last year to the twenty-fifth reunion of the Dutch Underground. We could never duplicate that trip. The Dutch people treated us so grandly. I looked forward to thanking as many people as I could for Owen's safe return. We were escorted all over Holland by Jan Ket. We visited Truida where she and her husband, Hendrick, lived in a new home on the same ground where Somsenhuis stood. I met Henk van t'Lam, Henk ten Have, Emmy Ket, Kokkie and *Dominee* Klijn, retired. The good Reverend obviously had cancer. His skin was pale and he looked very fragile. He died a few months after we returned home. There were so many people to see and so many to thank. In reality, they would not let us thank them, they wanted to thank us instead. They showered us with so many gifts that we were forced to send our own baggage home by freight so that there would be room in our suitcases for bare necessities and all their gifts.

    We saw many memorial statues while in Holland, but the most outstanding one was the statue erected in memory of the fifty-two Dutch hostages who were yanked from their homes and taken to a nearby field where they were shot, and no one was allowed to bury them. The blood from those sacrificed men and women caused the wheat that was grown there later to have a very large grain size. Some of the grain was placed in a glass enclosure that became part of the memorial, and is still there today.

    While in Holland, Owen, who accompanied Jan Ket to the celebration of the Queen at her summer palace which was only about two miles down the road from his home, was stopped by an American journalist who asked him why he was there. When he told him he had been taking a nostalgic trip around Holland which included the places he, himself, was hidden and taken care of by brave Dutch citizens, he asked if he could take the same trip with him so that he could make a photo-story about

Epilogue

him. Owen consented and a few months after returning home, Owen was featured on television. It was called 'Dutch Treat'.

    Henk, the eldest Prinzen, spoke as we turned onto a dirt road. "It is not far now. Moeder is waiting, and," he grinned, "she's been fluttering around like a butterfly ever since she knew you were coming."

    Just ahead was the reason we had traveled to this part of Canada. Owen had talked so much about the family who saved his life during the war, taking risks to make all those airmen as comfortable and safe as possible, that I was looking forward eagerly to meeting Dora Prinzen, who was now a widow and lived alone.

    Henk stopped the car in front of the porch and got out. He waved greetings to Moeder as he opened the door on my side, while Owen hopped out on the other side.

    She stood on the porch. Her hair had turned white since last Owen saw her, he said, but otherwise she looked much the same though she had to be in her early seventies. I clung to Owen's hand as we hurried up the front porch steps. Owen hugged the lovely lady and then introduced her to me. I planted a kiss on Dora's cheek, then spoke the only Dutch words I knew.

    "*Danka*, Moeder, God bless you!" There were sudden tears in Dora's blue eyes as she looked at me.

    She answered in a hushed voice, "*God zegene u*". Then smiling, she turned and opened the screen door and motioned us inside. Henk followed with our suitcases.

    After we settled in, we toured the big house. On the walls in the downstairs rooms were Dora's precious memories of the Prinzen family in Holland sent to her by friends and relatives. Pictures of the seven flyers who hid in their hayloft for several months were conspicuously displayed. Owen pointed out to me the names of all the people in the photos. I followed closely behind him asking questions. There were two awards for bravery, one from the Dutch Underground signed by the Queen of the Netherlands, and there was a framed letter of commendation signed by Dwight D. Eisenhower for the courageous role she and her family played during World War II.

Two more sons, Marinus and Derk, arrived and we sat around the kitchen table while they talked of the days at Somsenhuis. The memories were many and the babble went on for some time while I sat comfortably in a chair content to listen to the stories.

When the chatter died down, however, I leaned forward toward Dora and asked, "What happened after the war was over and my husband and the rest of the flyers left for their own homes? How was it with you?"

All conversation stopped. Dora rested her usually busy hands in her lap and gently rocked her chair. I recognized the signs. We were going to be treated to a little story. The light from the window gave a subtle glow to her face. Her soft, white hair was combed neatly into a knot at the back of her neck.

"We missed all of you very much," she began, "though nearly all of you wrote and sent things to us. There was hunger, unemployment, and destruction everywhere. It was better in the country where we lived than the cities." She sighed and straightened her shoulders and then continued. "Even little Benny, who was four, would have been included with all of us being charged with suspicion for helping the Allies. We were scheduled for the firing squad. Two more days and that would have happened.

"We all thanked God for our deliverance. Then we went to work. We planted a garden first, then cleaned the house from top to basement, but we forgot about the explosives in the hidden room in the hayloft where all the pilots slept.

"When the garden was about ready to use, a lightning storm struck early one evening and the roof burst into flames. Before we realized it, the house was on fire and the flames reached the ammunition and grenades. There was a series of explosions. We had only time to get out and save ourselves. Somsenhuis was destroyed leaving only the barn.

"We had the clothes we were wearing and we saved the old clock." She gestured toward the beautifully decorated clock ticking placidly on the wall above her head. "Again we thanked God for our survival. Since the barn was spared, Bernard and the boys began fixing it up for the family to live in. Meanwhile, we lived with my *moeder* and *vader* nearby. But from that time on, my Bernard was never very well. His spirit was broken. His strength was gone.

Epilogue

"One day, with a basket over my arm, I set out from my parents' farm to gather vegetables from our garden. I was sad and worried. Bernard was not well and the government had no money to loan us so that we could rebuild. There was no work and no future for the children. Even the bicycles and horses were gone. The Germans took everything. As I walked, tears ran down my face.

"After filling my basket with vegetables, I put the basket down and lay down between the rows of vegetables with the hot sun on my back. I rested my face on my arms and cried. One hand rested on a piece of wood lying in the dirt. It felt smooth under my palm. I rubbed it with my fingers and soon I raised my head to take a look at it. I sat up and rubbed it some more and polished it with my apron."

There were tears in Dora's eyes now as she continued. "I was still crying. My troubles were heavy. Then, I turned the piece of wood over to clean the other side. There were words on it: *VETROUWEN OP GOD*. I wiped the tears away and looked at the words again, and I realized I had not been leaving everything up to God. Some of the sadness left me. I picked up my basket and, holding the piece of polished wood close, I returned to my parents' home. I felt hope for the first time in weeks."

"What do the words mean!" I asked.

"Have faith in God," she answered. "It was a little sign that had hung on the wall at the farm. So we trusted in God. Later, we sold the farm and moved here to Ontario, Canada, where we've done very well. Bernard died in 1965," a fleeting look of pain and loss crossed her face, then she smiled, "but I have many beautiful grandchildren. Our oldest daughter and her husband bought back the farm.

"On the wall of the new Somsenhuis is the piece of polished wood I found in the garden that summer of 1945."

Authors' Notes
1995

Doris's Note

When the Prinzen family moved, they came under the sponsorship of a church in Holland and a farmer in Ontario. They were placed with a farm family in the Ontario area and all the older boys worked on that farm. They soon realized they were not making much headway by this method so they pooled their money, and after a time they had money enough to start a farm of their own. They all have done pretty well. Hendrick went to work for General Motors Corporation in Oshawa, Ontario, John started a business in auto repair, Willum bought a farm, Marinus and Derk also bought farms of their own. Through the years, they all raised their own families and Dora was blessed with many grandchildren. Little Benny, by the way, became the reeve of Prince Edward County (the equivalent of a mayor of a town) where he and his wife settled. We used to tease them and call it Prinzenville, since so many members of that family lived in close proximity of each other.

As for the girls, Truida married the boy who lived down the road from Somsenhuis. They eventually bought back the farm and she and her husband, Hendrick Lammers, raised a beautiful family of their own. Hermein settled outside the Toronto area not far from Moeder Prinzen and she and her husband ran a dairy farm and vegetable garden. Johanna married a young man, Tom Vos, and they lived most of their married life in the city of Toronto. Anna's husband worked for a power company, and lived in a beautiful pine forest when we visited them. Later they moved to Belleville, not far from Bloomfield. Incidentally, Hendrick's wife, Didy, and Anna's husband, Fred Hoven, are brother and sister.

Author's Notes

Owen's Note

Upon arriving back home in California, I heard on the news that General Model had committed suicide in April, 1945, after his troops, numbering over 300,000, surrendered to the Allies.

In the summer of 1945, we heard the bad news that Somsenhuis burned to the ground leaving only the barn. The Prinzens were in dire need as were most of the people of Holland. We sent what we could as did the other six airmen.

Index

=A=

Aalten, Holland   11(map), 45, 91, 115
Alligator   13, 138
Amersfoort, Holland   156
Arnhem, Holland   10(map), 13, 57, 60, 85, 102
Australia   5, 15, 24, 103, 104, 105, 108, 146, 147

=B=

B-17 bomber   13, 14, 15, 23, 25, 38, 49, 142, 143, 148
Bake, Miss   21, 37-40, 43
Baker, Mr.   115
Barker, Mr.   113
bazooka   13, 51, 103, 120, 122
BBC   13, 62, 63, 114, 129, 156
Bedford, Walter   56
Belgium   15, 32, 129
Belleville, Canada   4, 161
Berlin   56
Black Jan   see Ket, Jan
Blackies   51
Bloomfield, Canada   157, 161
Boles, Todd   24
Bomber Command   3
Boyle, Fl.Lt.   105, 106
Bren gun   13, 51, 54, 87, 103
Brighton, England   23, 55, 105
British Columbia, Canada   147

Brown, Bobby. USAAF   21, 23, 28, 48, 49, 50, 51, 53, 55, 69-88, 89, 90, 94-97, 99, 117, 118, 120, 123, 130, 131, 138, 146, 149, 150-155

=C=

Camp Miles Standish, U.S.A.   105
Can Do Bomb Group   13, 26
C-47 aircraft   13, 139
California, U.S.A   3, 23, 24, 33, 44, 87, 92, 98, 141, 146, 149, 150, 154, 157, 162
Canada   2, 3, 5, 24, 146, 148, 157, 158, 160
Canadian Army   85, 102, 137, 145
Carnarvon, Wales   105
CeeBees   14, 144
Colt 45 pistol   14, 67, 70, 120

=D=

D-Day   4
Davis, Joe. USAAF   21, 23, 48, 49, 51, 55, 61-68, 95, 96, 99, 118, 124, 146
De Brink, Hans   38
De Bark   53(photo), 66, 68, 103, 118, 119, 122, 123, 135, 156

Dell, Frank. RAF   21, 23, 48, 49, 50,
  55, 56-68, 89, 90, 92, 95, 96,
  97, 100, 103, 104, 117, 118,
  123, 124, 132, 133, 134, 137,
  139, 146, 148, 149-155
Den Dolder, Holland   148, 156
Dinxperlo, Holland   11(map), 116
Dortmund-Ems Canal, Germany   106
Douglas, Wing Commander   106
Dutch Resistance   see Underground

=E=

Eisenhower   158
Eighth (8th) Air Force   3, 13
Escapee Society   146

=F=

Fieseler Storch aircraft   14, 102
Flying Fortress (B-17) aircraft   13, 14, 26
Focke-Wulf aircraft   13, 14, 56
Frankfurt, Germany   156
French Resistance   50

=G=

Gestapo   14, 93, 109, 123
Gaanderen, Holland   148
General Motors Corporation   161
GI Bill of Rights   14, 147
Greenock, Scotland   105

=H=

Harley-Davidson motorcycle   54
Harmsen, J.H.   21, 117, 127
Hereford, Keith   28
Hettinga, Co   21, 47, 93, 102, 104,
  117, 148
Hoenlo, Castle   44
Horger, Tom   25, 28
Hossidy, Colonel   155
Hoven, Fred and Didy   161
Huntley, Chuck. RCAF   24, 117, 118,
  19, 122, 125-127, 139, 147

=J=

Janson, Tor   59
Jewish family   44

=K=

Karlsruhe, Germany   56
Ket, Jan (Black Jan)   21, 22, 53, 54,
  62, 65, 66, 67, 87, 92-95, 97,
  98, 99, 101, 102, 103, 117,
  120, 121, 123, 132, 138, 148,
  155, 156, 157
Klijn, *Dominee*   97, 98, 157

=L=

Lammers, Hendrick and Truida   161
Lancaster bomber   14, 24, 56, 105,
  117, 125
Long Henk   see Van t'Lam, Henk
Luftwaffe   14, 129
Luger pistol   14, 47, 51, 78

=M=

Market Garden, operation   13
Mauser rifle   14, 93
Mayberry, Candace Joan (Candy)   2, 3, 5, 142, 143, 144, 150
Mayberry, Doris   2, 3, 141-145, 150, 151, 154, 161
Mayberry, Owen. USAAF   2, 3, 5, 23, 25-35, 96, 141-145, 147-158, 162
Mayberry, Thurman   141, 142
Messerschmitt aircraft   13, 14, 56
Messing, Terry   27, 28
Milwaukee, Wisconsin   44, 147
Misburg, Germany   25, 143
Model   102, 162
Moody Field, Georgia   23
Mosquito aircraft   14, 56, 57
Münster, Germany   57, 69
Mustang (P-51) aircraft   15, 27, 68, 69

=N=

Naiff, Ron   56
Nijmegen, Holland   10(map), 85
Normandy   4

=O=

Olst, Holland   10(map), 45, 148
Overmars, Toni and Herman   21, 44, 148

=P=

P-47 aircraft   15, 27
P-51 aircraft   see Mustang

Paris   139, 145
Parks, Australia   105
Port Pirie, Australia   105
Prince Bernhard   155
Prince Edward County, Canada   3, 4, 5, 161
Prinzen family   1-5, 19, 48, 49 52, 53, 55, 62, 88(photo), 89, 91, 96, 98, 101, 118, 122, 123, 129, 132, 135, 146, 147, 148, 158, 161, 162
   Bernard (Papa)   19(photo), 22, 48, 68, 88-93, 97, 99, 100, 103, 123, 130-133, 137, 148
   Dora (Moeder)   19(photo), 22, 42, 48, 52, 68, 88, 89, 90, 93, 101, 103, 133, 147, 148, 158, 161

=Q=

Quislings   41, 62, 89

=R=

RAF (Royal Air Force)   15, 23, 55, 111, 137
Red Cross   74, 142, 143
Roblee, Ted. USAAF   24, 25, 28, 36-51, 55, 62, 64, 66, 68, 90, 94, 96, 97, 118, 123, 133, 147, 154
Roleinhurst, Germany   125
Romboy, Fl.Sgt.   126
Ruhr Valley, Germany   105

=S=

Saskatchewan, Canada   24, 147
Schmidt, Henry   24, 26, 28

Smolders, Miss   21, 37-40, 43
Somsenhuis farm   21, 46-55, 62, 65,
    67, 68, 88, 89-95, 103, 116,
    119, 123, 127, 138, 147, 148,
    157, 159-162
Sontink, Mr.   21, 43, 44
Sten gun   15, 51, 87, 98, 103, 119, 120
Sterling bomber   15, 64
Strickland, Jim. RAAF   21, 24, 103,
    104, 105-116, 118, 119, 121,
    122, 132, 139, 147
Student, General   102

=T=

Te Brink, Ben   92
Toronto, Canada   161
Typhoon aircraft   15, 102

=U=

Undergound (Dutch Resistance)   1, 21,
    22, 45, 53, 54, 62, 66, 73, 83,
    85-88, 91-94, 97, 98, 99, 101-104,
    111, 115-122, 129, 135, 146,
    156, 157, 158
USAAF   13, 15, 23

=V=

V-1 bomb   15, 44
V-2 rocket   15, 32, 41

Van Limburg Stirum, Count S.J.   21,
    45-48, 148
Van Lom, Henry   84-87

Van t'Lam, Hendrick (Long Henk)   21,
    53, 99, 148, 157
Van t'Lam, Kokkie   99, 157
Varsseveld, Holland   11(map), 112, 115
Veenendahl, Mr.   45
Vos, Tom   161

=W=

Wellington aircraft   15, 105
Weocyewski, Leo   28
Wesepe, Holland   11(map), 29, 148
Willson, Bob   28
Winterswijk, Holland   11(map), 110,
    111

=Z=

Zuider Zee, Holland   10(map), 27, 156
Zutphen, Holland   10(map), 45
Zwarte Jan   see Ket, Jan

SEVEN ON A MAT

by Doris Mayberry
with Owen Mayberry

© 2020 Candace Joan Mayberry

All rights reserved. No part of this publication may be reproduced, stored in a retrieval system or transmitted in any form or by any means, electronic, mechanical, photocopying recording or otherwise without the prior written consent of the copyright holder.

www.ingramcontent.com/pod-product-compliance
Lightning Source LLC
Chambersburg PA
CBHW070427010526
44118CB00014B/1941